# THE ART OF BOBBIN LACE

# THE ART OF BOBBIN LACE

## A Practical Text Book of Workmanship

ILLUSTRATED
WITH ORIGINAL DESIGNS IN ITALIAN, POINT DE FLANDRE
BRUGES GUIPURE, DUCHESSE, HONITON, "RAISED"
HONITON, APPLIQUÉ, AND BRUXELLES

Also How to Clean and Repair Valuable Lace, etc.

BY

## LOUISA A. TEBBS

Facsimile Edition
TO WHICH ARE ADDED RECENTLY
DISCOVERED PATTERNS PREPARED
BY THE AUTHOR

COMBINED ONE VOLUME EDITION
PUBLISHED BY
PAUL P. B. MINET
SACKVILLE STREET, LONDON, W.1.
1978

Reprinted in 1978 by
Paul P. B. Minet, Piccadilly Rare Books Ltd.,
30 Sackville Street, London,W1X 1DB


Originally published in 1907 by
Chapman and Hall Ltd., London



SBN 85609 027 1

*Printed in Great Britain by*
The Scolar Press Limited, Ilkley, Yorkshire

# CONTENTS

# LIST OF ILLUSTRATIONS *

\* *Several original patterns have been added to this edition, reproduced on two folding sheets at the back. They correspond to illustrations marked by an asterisk.*

# INTRODUCTORY

On the charm of Lace it is scarcely necessary to dwell; it is prized by every woman and is the only ornament that is always suitable and becoming from infancy to old age, whilst in its unobtrusive elegance it lends a beauty and dignity to the wearer which raises her at once above the ordinary level.

Lace-making may certainly be classed under the Fine Arts, especially when allied to good design, for it must be remembered that, like most of the Fine Arts, design plays a very important part in Lace, and it was mainly due to the lack of good designs that our English Lace Industry diminished so seriously.

A great effort is being made to revive it, however, and when the matter is properly understood, which is merely a question of time, this revival of one of our oldest and most interesting industries will receive the encouragement necessary for its future prosperity. Belgium in particular has set us a good example in this respect, Lace-making in that country being a great national Industry, and no doubt Belgium owes much of her present prosperity to this revived and ever-increasing Lace Industry, whilst in many of the Continental towns and villages it is regarded as so useful

B

an accomplishment that the art of Lace-making is taught in the public elementary schools.

Every girl, rich or poor, should be taught Bobbin Lace; it is most fascinating work, the movement of the bobbins being so different to anything else, and it is neither tedious nor trying to the eyes, a great point.

" There is still," says Ruskin, " some distinction between Machine-made and Hand-made Lace.   I will suppose that distinction so far done away with that, a pattern once invented, you can spin Lace as fast as they now do thread. Everybody then might wear, not only Lace collars, but Lace gowns.   Do you think that, when everybody could wear them, everybody would be proud of wearing them ?   A spider may, perhaps, be rationally proud of his own cobweb, even though all the fields in the morning are covered with the like, for he made it himself ;  but suppose a machine spun it for him ? suppose all the gossamer were Nottingham made ?   If you think of it, you will find the whole value of Lace as a possession depends on the fact of its having a *beauty* which has been the reward of industry and attention. That the thing is itself a price—a thing everybody cannot have.   That it proves, by the look of it, the ability of the maker ; that it proves, by the rarity of it, the dignity of its wearer.   The real good of a piece of Lace, then, you will find, is that it should show first, that the designer of it had a pretty fancy ; next, that the maker of it had fine fingers ; and lastly, that the wearer of it has worthiness or dignity enough to obtain what it is difficult to obtain."

To the nervous delicate woman, the making of Bobbin Lace is a restful, soothing occupation, and in these days of stress and strain, it would prove a complete boon if every woman gave a few hours' relaxation daily to this beautiful art, whilst ladies with benevolent intentions would find it a lucrative and suitable occupation to introduce into Homes and Charitable Institutions, especially for crippled children, invalids of either sex, and others requiring a light, interesting occupation, that can be followed with very little outlay and expense.

The term " Bobbin " Lace is a very comprehensive one, there being over fifty varieties, most of them demanding different treatment, for although the three principal stitches commonly known as Cloth Stitch, Half Stitch and Plait Stitch form the foundation of all kinds of Bobbin Lace, yet in the application of these stitches to the different kinds of Lace, the method varies considerably.

After making a thorough study of the different branches, and analyzing as it were the whole theory of Lace-making, I came to the conclusion that to the *worker* Bobbin Lace may be divided broadly into two classes, which I will call, (1) Sectional, (2) Continuous, the meaning being that the first-named variety is worked in sections, the fancy fillings and connecting bars being put in separately, (before removing the lace from the cushion), requiring about eighteen bobbins *only* (often less) for the most elaborate patterns. This class comprises some of the most beautiful laces, including Italian Point de Flandre, Bruge Guipure, Duchesse, Honiton, Bruxelles, &c.

As it is with the Sectional class of lace only that I propose to deal in this book, I will not do more than point out the difference in the two species. To begin with, in the Continuous variety, the entire pattern is worked across at once, completing the lace row by row as you proceed. Now you will understand to do this a great many bobbins are necessary, so that for quite a narrow simple pattern forty bobbins would be required, and for an elaborate pattern any number up to 600.

The making of this class of Lace (which includes Torchon, Maltese, Valenciennes, Buckinghamshire, Bedfordshire, Mechlin, &c.) is therefore unavoidably more complicated and difficult (though also, once a pattern is mastered, more mechanical) and I do not advise any one to attempt these laces until they are proficient in the Sectional variety.

I think the reason that most people have such an exaggerated impression of the difficulties of Bobbin Lace is that they invariably start with these complicated branches first, and in every case that has come under my notice of unsuccessful and discouraging attempts to master this art, I have traced all failures chiefly to this source.

As this book is intended for a practical help and instructor, not only to those taking up Bobbin Lace as an accomplishment, but also to those desiring to adopt it as a profession (and I believe there is a good opening for qualified teachers in many parts of England and elsewhere), it may interest and benefit these latter, and I hope will not be considered presumptuous on my part if I give a general explanation of my own system of teaching, which, after careful study and *remembering my own difficulties*, I have adopted.

FIRST.    It should be borne in mind that it is advisable from the very beginning to encourage the pupils to rely whenever possible on their own intuition and intelligence, avoiding all mechanism ; this is one of the reasons why—contrary to all established rule—I discard pricked patterns for all the so-called Sectional Laces. The design should be carefully sketched out, showing all working details, and the pupil trained to regulate her own pin pricks as she makes the lace ; she will thus accustom herself to suit the placing of the pins exactly to her own individual work, which varies a little in every case.

SECOND.    The patterns for each course should be designed in sets progressively, commencing with the very simplest, and contriving that not only is something new learnt at each lesson, but also that it contains practice of everything learnt in the previous lessons; the different branches of lace too, should follow systematically in the progressing stages of difficulty, so that although each branch is a complete study in itself, it is also a help towards the next branch.

In this way I find the pupils continue to progress without any undue effort, whilst the fascination and interest of making really beautiful and at the same time useful specimens of lace from the beginning, which can be turned to good account, adds a zeal and interest which increases with each lesson.

It is too often overlooked that a rule does not hold good in every case, and the teaching must therefore in a great measure be adapted to circumstances; a case in point is the making of certain kinds of Sectional Lace in separate pieces, when for a single collar or flounce the worker prepares dozens of separate flowers, leaves, scrolls, &c., which afterwards she arranges, pins down again on a cushion and connects all together.

A moment's thought will show that while this method may be a time-saver to the wholesale manufacturer, it proves the very opposite to the ordinary lace-maker and should be strictly avoided. A far better plan, and one that encourages individual artistic effort, is to teach the pupil to complete the lace as she goes on, thereby saving time and seeing the effect of the work as she proceeds; and all patterns should be arranged for this method.

Now if Bobbin Lace is taught scientifically, any girl or woman of ordinary intelligence can with a few hours' practice daily acquire the art in a very short time, and it may be an encouragement to mention that in my own personal experience as a teacher, which is a large and varied one, including students in many grades of life and ages varying from ten to sixty years, I have never known a pupil leave off through discouragement or inability.

It is in a great measure owing to this apparent proof of the simplicity and interest of Lace-making, and to ensure a wider enthusiasm for this beautiful art, that I have been persuaded to write this book, and also to encourage those pupils (whose names are legion) that come to me from long distances and far-off countries, and whose time in many cases does not allow them to learn more than one or two branches, but are very anxious to proceed further, to these I hope it will prove a special benefit as well as to the beginner.

It will be understood that it is impossible here in a book of this size to give my full sets of patterns for working out each branch, but I have endeavoured to select the most helpful and beautiful variety, all of which, with one or two exceptions, I have designed specially for the purpose, whilst each specimen has been worked out under my personal supervision, so that everything reproduced is thoroughly practical and correct in each working detail, and though this volume cannot pretend to be exhaustive, the student, after studying this little book and carefully following the directions given, will have no difficulty in reproducing these specimens, step by step as given, and after she has accomplished this will then find she has a very comprehensive knowledge of some of the most beautiful forms of Bobbin Lace.

In conclusion, I should like to encourage all students of lace to make their own designs; the work has then a double interest for them. So many women I find lack the initiative, not through any want of intelligence or ability, but simply through not having been trained and accustomed to observe beautiful forms and reproduce them.

LOUISA A. TEBBS.

Ivory
Bobbins.

Boxwood
Bobbins.

Ivory
Bobbins.

Lace
Pricker.

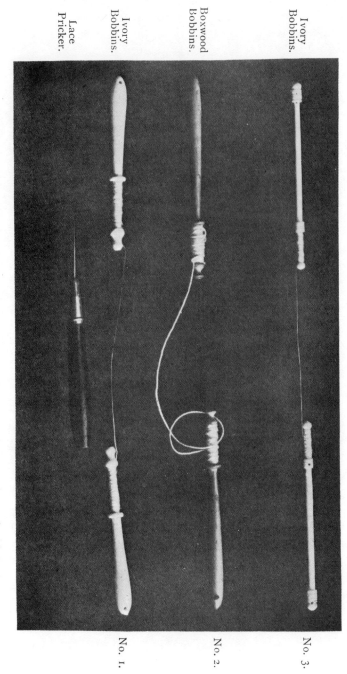

No. 3.

No. 2.

No. 1.

Illustration of the three styles of Bobbins used for making all the Lace specimens in this book.

# THE ART OF BOBBIN LACE

## IMPORTANT HINTS

A SMALL "mushroom" cushion is the best for working all these Sectional laces upon (the padding of which must be *perfectly even*), slightly raised in the centre, tapering towards the sides, with a flat solid foundation, whilst the bobbins should be the shape of the illustrations on page 2, the ivory bobbins taking precedence over the wooden variety as being prettier to look at, pleasanter to handle, and emitting a more decided clicking sound as they glide quickly into place, than the wooden bobbins, though for practical purposes these latter are just as good.

Nos. 1 and 2 bobbins are suitable for all the different kinds of lace in this book—No. 3 for any of the "Fillings" or for working entire lace in the No. 4 thread only.

Lace-makers will find it a great convenience to have an extra set or two of bobbins in reserve wound ready for use, thereby saving a great deal of time and trouble, particularly when working the more elaborate patterns where extra bobbins are required for all the fancy " Fillings."

The Flemish thread, specially soft and strong, is to be recommended in preference to the ordinary linen threads, (which are too harsh for this variety of lace,) the sizes used for the illustrated specimens are Nos. 1, 2, 3, 4, with cords to correspond. The pins must be fine and tapering and are " silvered " to prevent rust.

Whilst the lace is in progress it should be covered with a transparent linen cover in which a round opening about one inch in diameter has been cut out of the middle—this enables the lace-maker to see the part she is working, prevents the catching of the pins in the parts already worked, and also keeps the lace clean. It is perhaps as well to remark at this point that all Bobbin Lace is worked *with the wrong side outwards and the right side next to the cushion*—this enables the worker to arrange her commencing, connecting, or fastening-off threads more easily, and keeps the right side perfectly neat.

A " pricker " is also a very useful instrument for lace workers, and should be kept handy for stroking and arranging the threads into position occasionally whilst the lace is in progress, undoing knots, &c.

6

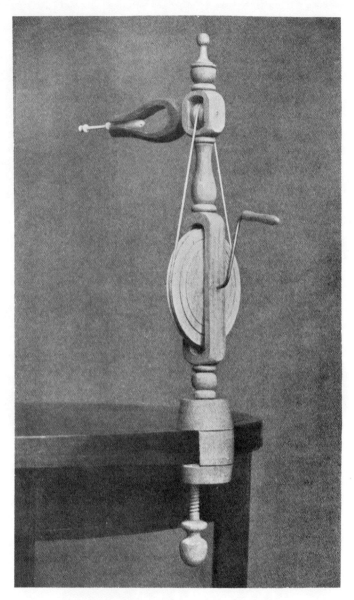

Showing the Bobbin Winder with a bobbin in position ready for filling.

## PREPARING THE BOBBINS

Tie the thread firmly to the bobbin, which either place in your Bobbin Winder, or wind by hand until nearly full, when all are ready they must be fastened together in pairs, which is done as follows :—Take up two filled bobbins, tie the ends of the threads together in an ordinary knot, trim neatly, and wind about two yards of thread past this knot on one of the pair only, wind up until they are three inches apart, and secure the thread on each bobbin with a slip knot or half hitch made by forming a loop in the thread and putting the head of the bobbin through this loop. (See illustration, page 2.)

## THE PATTERNS

Too much stress cannot be laid on having a properly prepared pattern, as it is quite impossible to make good lace on an imperfectly drawn or inaccurate pattern, and it is also necessary that all the special points are carefully marked. Designing for Bobbin Lace is a branch to itself, and though not difficult to master, it certainly needs a course of study.

c

"Cloth" Stitch.  "Half" Stitch.  "Plait" Stitch.

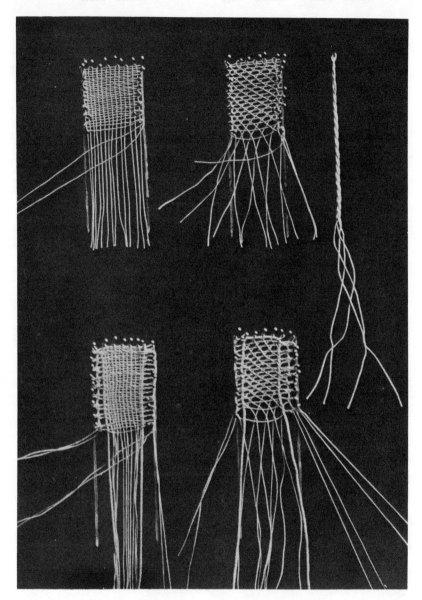

"Cloth" Stitch with    "Half" Stitch with
"Open edge" and "Picots."    "Open edge" and "Picots."

## "ITALIAN" LACE EDGE.

We will begin with the simplest of all Bobbin Laces, viz. Italian, and as the style of this lace does not offer much scope and variety of design, we will, after mastering this effective and useful little pattern, pass on to the more elaborate varieties.

You will require six pairs of bobbins for this design, filled with No. 1 thread, and tied together in pairs as described on page 7, and a packet of " medium " lace pins.

Stick three pins in the dots indicated in the pattern. Hang two pairs of bobbins on the right-hand pin, and make a "Cloth" stitch, which is done as follows with four bobbins (for greater clearness we will number these bobbins 1, 2, 3, 4, counting from the right): cross No. 3 bobbin over No. 2, No. 1 over No. 2, No. 3 over No. 4, and No. 3 over No. 2, assuming, of course, that the bobbins change their number as they move, i.e. the pair nearest the right hand being always No. 1, and so on.

After this stitch is worked leave the right-hand pair of bobbins, hang a new pair on the next pin, and work a

"Cloth" stitch with the left-hand pair and the new pair, and so on until the whole six pairs are worked (two pairs on each pin); now make a "Picot" as follows:—Twist the outer pair of bobbins three times to the left, put a pin under this thread, giving the pin an extra twist round the thread before pinning down; make a "Cloth" stitch with the two outside pairs, repeating the four movements exactly the same as before. Now twist each of these two pairs twice to the left,* leave the outside or left-hand pair and work a "Cloth" stitch with the inner pair and the next, and so on, until all except the last pair are worked, and before making this stitch twist each of the two last pairs twice to the left, stick a pin in *front* of both pairs of bobbins, making a "Cloth" stitch at the back of the pin, twist both pairs twice again, leave the outer or right-hand pair and work across with the inner pair as before, until all except the last stitch is worked. See that both pairs are twisted twice before working this stitch, then twist (the outer pair only) three times for the "Picot." Pin down as before, make a second "Cloth" stitch and twist each pair twice again to the left and repeat from* and so on until you arrive at the first "Strand" A, which you must throw out as follows (remembering that the "Picots" only occur on the outline of the lace and that the braid is

13

"Italian" Lace edge.

For full-size pattern see folding sheet 1.

worked both edges alike in the parts where the " Picots "
cease):—

After completing the row at point A, stick a pin in
the opposite end of the strand B, twist your outer pair
of bobbins nearest the strand eight times, hang this
twisted thread round the pin and back again, making a
" Cloth " stitch with this pair and the next, stick another
pin in between these two pairs of bobbins and work another
" Cloth " stitch round the pin, twist each pair twice to
the left and proceed as before, throwing out strand C in
the same manner.

These strands must be taken up into the lace at the
other side. To do this, when you arrive at the pin on
which the strand was made, take out the pin and insert a
crochet hook through the strand, pull the thread of the
nearest bobbin through this strand until a large loop is
formed, and pass the second bobbin through this loop,
pull tight, make a " Cloth " stitch, put the pin back again,
make another " Cloth " stitch round the pin, twist each pair
of bobbins twice and proceed with the ordinary braid as
before, connecting every row now on this side of the braid
which comes close to that already worked by taking out
the pin and drawing the thread of your nearest bobbin
through the edge of the braid as for the strand.

N.B.—The pins should be placed *quite close* together on the *inner* side of all curves, and the outer pins regulated to come as nearly opposite the inner pins as possible.

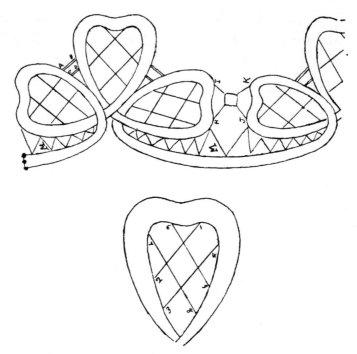

When you have worked the length of your pattern—or as far as you conveniently can—on your cushion, leave all your working bobbins (taking the precaution to keep these in place by stretching a wide piece of elastic tightly over the bobbins, securing it to the cushion with large pins) and put in your "Fillings" and "Strands" with four separate bobbins tied together in pairs as previously described, and work as follows :—Take out the pin at 1, insert a crochet hook where the pin has been, and draw the thread of one pair of bobbins (through the edge of the braid) into a large loop; put one of the bobbins through this loop and pull tight. Insert another pair in the same place, in the same manner, and work "Plait" stitch which is done as follows :—

Cross No. 3 bobbin over No. 2, 1 over 2, 3 over 4, 3 over 2, 1 over 2, 3 over 4, and so on until you arrive at 2, where you take out the nearest pin and connect to the lace as described before; continue the plait stitch to 3, connect again to the lace and work across to 4, then to 5 and 6, 7, and 8. When you arrive at 8 tie each pair of bobbins together in four tight knots, reversing the tie each time and cut off close.

The "strands" in space M are worked in the same way, the little "Picots" that occur at intervals in all the "Plait" stitch strands being formed by simply twisting a pin round the thread of the nearest bobbin and pinning it down whenever you arrive at a dot which indicates a "Picot."

The "Spider Webs" that connect the "Bows" together are also worked with *two pairs* of bobbins, each pair after being connected to the lace (one pair at J and a pair at K), are twisted until they reach the middle, then hung over two pins, one at each corner of the little square; three bobbins are held in the left hand, the fourth bobbin being used as a shuttle weaving over and under the other threads until a square centre is formed; a pin is stuck in each of the lower corners, and a pair of bobbins hung over each pin; the threads are then twisted up to the opposite side of the lace H and I, where they are connected, tied together, and cut off.

Although, when once the knack is acquired, these effective little " Spider Webs" are very quickly and easily made, it requires a certain amount of practice to obtain this knack, and beginners must not be discouraged if at first they cannot get them perfect.

The next step after completing the " Fillings and Strands" is to take out all the pins from the lace and remove it from the pattern, fitting the part you are working carefully on the beginning of the pattern at the top of the cushion, secure with a few pins, straighten out your working bobbins—which will have become a little entangled in the process—and proceed.

## DOYLEY IN DENTELLE DE BRUGES
### (POINT DE FLANDRE)

We will now attempt the next easiest branch of Bobbin Lace, commonly known as Point de Flandre (or to be technically correct, Dentelle de Bruges); this fascinating lace is comparatively very easy of execution and admits of much more variety of design. I should suggest the Doyley on page 21 for the first attempt, then the Collar on page 28 (or the Lace Edge on page 32), and lastly the more elaborate *Motifs* on page 36.

Have ready eight pairs of bobbins filled with No. 2 thread, each pair tied together and wound up to within three inches apart (as described on page 7) you will also require one bobbin filled with Bruges cord—the cord outline being one of the characteristics of this lace—and a packet of "medium" lace pins.

To begin, stick three pins in the ring of one of the flowers (as indicated by the black dots) and hang on eight pairs of bobbins, one pair only at a time; work "Cloth" stitch right across, commencing from the inner side of the ring ; stick a pin on the outer edge of the ring in *front* of the two last pairs just worked, twist each pair twice to the left, now make a knot in your outline cord and pin it down about one inch away ; pass this cord through the second or inner pair of bobbins (over one bobbin, under the next) and leave it between this and the outside pair ; now work " Cloth " stitch across with this same pair of bobbins until all except the last pair are worked, twist this pair twice, also

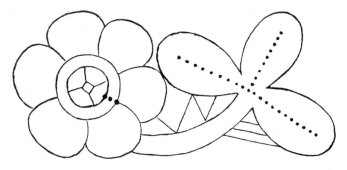

the working pair twice (to the left), stick a pin in *front* of these four bobbins and make a " Cloth " stitch at the back of the pin which will now be on the inner side of the ring ; twist each pair twice again and return with the inner pair, working " Cloth " stitch right across until you arrive at the cord ; pass this through your working pair, twist this pair twice, stick a pin in *front* and make a " Cloth " stitch with this and the outside pair at the back of the pin, twist both pairs twice, work across with the inner pair the same

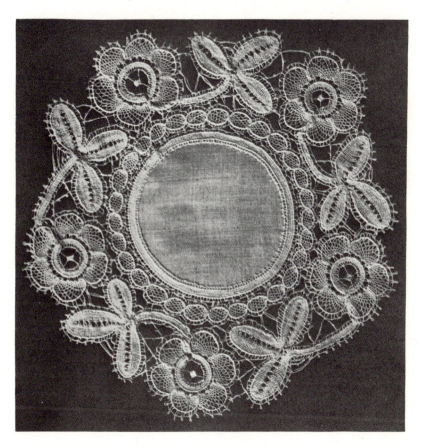

Doyley in Dentelle de Bruges.
(Point de Flandre.)

For full-size pattern see folding sheet 2.

as last row, repeating the directions given row for row. To
connect the ring together at the finish take out the inner
starting pin, insert a fine crochet hook and draw the thread
of the nearest bobbin through the opening, put the next
bobbin right through the loop just formed and pull tight ;
work to the middle of ring and repeat, also at the outer
edge, so that the ring is connected together in all three
places ; now work " Half " stitch right across the petal ; to do
this first cross every pair of bobbins *once to the left.* This
being done, take up the first two pairs and *cross the *two
inner bobbins* once to the right, cross each of these two
pairs once to the left again, drop the outer pair, take
up the next pair and repeat from* work all except
the last pair, and, before doing this, cross the working
pair once to the left, pass the cord through these crossed
threads ; now stick a pin at the top of the petal and
with the two outer pairs of bobbins work a " Cloth " stitch
round this pin, leave the outer pair, pass the cord through the
inner pair and work back in " Half " stitch. Connect when
you arrive at the ring of the flower, make a " Cloth " stitch
after the connection to hold it firm, and then work " Half "
stitch across until all except the last pair is worked;
pass the cord through the last pair but one (previously
crossed to the left), twist both these outside pairs twice,
at the back of the pin, stick a pin in *front* of these bobbins

and make a " Cloth " stitch, twist each pair twice again ; drop the outer pair, pass the cord through the inner pair and work "Half" stitch right across, including the last pair, remembering to connect again to the ring ; make a " Cloth " stitch and repeat these last two rows until all the six petals are worked, threading the cord down to the ring and back again, at the division of each.

These petals are connected together at the finish the same as the ring, working this *last row* in " Cloth " stitch to hold the connections firm.

The stalk of the leaves is worked exactly the same as the circle of the flower. The leaves are also worked in " Cloth " stitch with the same open edge and cord all round the outside of the leaf, but to form the vein, work across to the dots (up the middle of the leaf) with plain " Cloth " stitch up to the very last pair ; after this pair is worked, stick a pin in *the vein*, take the outer pair of bobbins round this pin and twist (this pair only) twice, before working back ; this is done every row until the top of the vein is reached, then work round the other side of the leaf, connecting the vein in the middle as follows :—

After the top of the vein is reached, continue to work the same Stitch round the tip of leaf, but *without any pins or twistings* on the *inner side* until you arrive opposite the top pin in the vein; take this pin out and connect with the crochet hook as described in the flower, remembering now to twist the outer pair of bobbins once before and once after these connections to match the double twistings on the opposite side. Work round the second and third sections of the leaf in the same manner, when the bobbins must be fastened off; to do this take the whole of the bobbins in the left hand, except one; with this one bobbin tie the others together in a tight buttonhole stitch. About six of these stitches are sufficient to make the fastening very secure. Now cut off the bobbins quite close and wind up in pairs as previously described. If the little extra precaution is taken at the finish of sewing these fastenings neatly down on the wrong side, the lace will never give way in cleaning as is so often the case.

For the small "Half" stitch circles round the doyley two cords are used, one each side. The bobbins containing these cords are tied together and wound up like the others, and when commencing these circles the pair of cord bobbins should be hung round the commencing pins after the others have all been worked on.

These circles are worked in "Half" stitch with the usual "open edge," but at each division the cords are crossed as follows: after putting in your pin at this point (and twice

D

twisting the two outer pairs of bobbins) *before passing your cord through the inner pair as usual, thread this cord over and under all the other bobbins until it reaches the opposite cord, leave it and bring this opposite cord back in the same manner,* now pass it through the pair of bobbins you were about to work with and proceed as usual.

After connecting the circles together at the finish, the bobbins must be fastened off and cut close as for the leaf, then wound up in pairs ready for the inner circle of braid round the doyley. This is worked exactly the same as the ring in the flower, using one cord only on the outer edge of the braid.

Remember in working this lace to connect all parts of the design that come close to each other, by simply inserting the crochet hook and drawing the nearest working bobbin through, as described before.

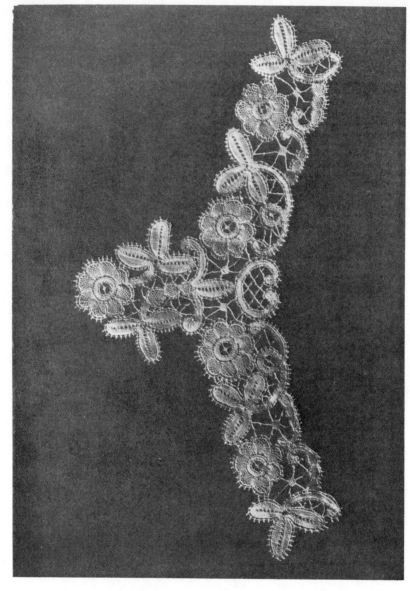

Collar in Dentelle de Bruges.

## COLLAR IN DENTELLE DE BRUGES

This pretty little collar might be attempted first instead of the doyley if preferred.

Work the flowers, leaves, &c., the same as the doyley, also the connecting strands and the small woven " Spider-Webs " in the centre of the flowers. For the large "Spider-Webs," however, that connect the flowers and leaves, you will require *six pairs* of bobbins,—two pairs for each of the three strands at the top of the " Web." Work these three strands as usual in " Plait " stitch with a " Picot " in the middle of each ; when the third strand is finished stick a pin at the corner of the solid square nearest this strand and work a " Cloth " stitch round the pin, drop the outer pair of bobbins and work another " Cloth " stitch, taking up the nearest pair of bobbins from the next strand, repeat with the next pair and so on until you have worked a row of " Cloth " stitches right across—stick a pin in the opposite corner to the first pin and work·a " Cloth " stitch round this

pin—work " Cloth " stitch across, repeat for about six rows
or until the little square is large enough, then work the two
outer pairs each side in " Plait " stitch, and also the two
middle pairs until they reach their destination, where
connect, tie firmly together and cut off close.

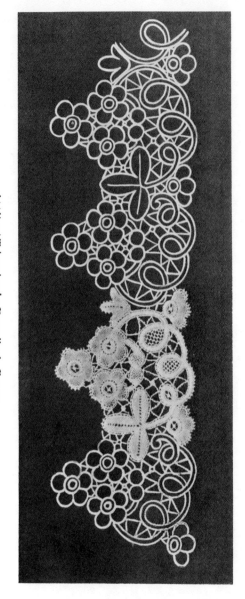

*Appliqué* Trimming in Dentelle de Bruges.

## *APPLIQUÉ* TRIMMING IN DENTELLE DE BRUGES

This handsome lace, five inches deep, is suitable for a great many purposes, and can be worked in fine or coarse thread accordingly. The specimen illustrated is worked in No. 2 thread. Commence with the flower nearest the long curved stem, arranging that you finish with the petal nearest to this stem, continue to work the stem without cutting off the bobbins, but fasten on an extra cord here as the stem is worked with a cord each side, this extra cord must be cut off on arriving at the leaf (which is also continued out of the stem with the same bobbins), but you will find it necessary to put on two extra pairs of bobbins for the leaf; to do this work a few rows until you come to where the leaf slightly widens and hang an extra pair of bobbins on the outer pin of the last row *before passing your cord*: make a "Cloth" stitch with this new pair and the working pair—pass the cord, twist twice, pin as usual, and the next time you arrive at this outer edge of the leaf, hang on another pair in the same manner, taking care to now lift the previous pair off the pin and pull up tight.

The working of the pretty Reseau filling in the circles formed by the stem is described on page 53.

*Motifs* in Dentelle de Bruges. ("Butterfly," "Fan," "Lovers' Knot," and "Rose.")
Approximate size of each 4 × 3 inches.

For patterns of "Butterfly" and "Fan" see folding sheet 1.

## *MOTIFS* IN DENTELLE DE BRUGES

### "LOVERS' KNOT," "BUTTERFLY," "FAN" AND CONVENTIONAL ROSE

These dainty little *Motifs* form pretty ornaments for Hats, Blouses, &c., or set quite close together they make a handsome border for Collars and various articles arranged as fancy dictates.

To work the "Lovers' Knot," follow the direction given in the Italian insertion except that two cords are used, one each side—begin at the extreme point and work all the whole bow in one piece, fasten off neatly and cut close, tie the bobbins in pairs again and work the little centre in "Half" stitch.

For the "Butterfly," work the body first, commencing where it joins the top wing; work all round this and continue the upper wings without leaving off, first one wing, then the other—now continue the lower wing which is worked one half in "Cloth" stitch with a vein up the middle (as the leaf described in the doyley) and the opposite side in "Half" stitch, connecting each row to the vein as you proceed.

For the "Fan" *Motif*, work the flower first, finishing

at the petal nearest the braid on the left hand, and continue to work this braid all round, continuing the little open space between the fan and the ribbon by wrapping all the other bobbins with the two outside bobbins, tying them tight and connecting this tying pair to the edge of the flower, repeat this three times, straighten out the bobbins and proceed to work the ribbon.

The *"Flower" Motif* should be commenced on the inside ring close to the stem, work this and join together, continue round the whole of the seven petals (working the three middle petals in " Half " stitch)—also down the stem, then wrap and tie your bobbins together, connecting each tie until you reach the small scroll on the left-hand side of the stem, continue to work this scroll, and when finished fasten the bobbins off neatly, cut close, tie up in pairs, connect each pair to the stem and work the little scroll opposite ; after this second scroll is worked, the bobbins must be again cut off and tied up in pairs ready for the leaf, the open petals of the flower are filled in with the little woven " Spider Webs," and the middle of the ring with " Plaited " filling. Full directions for working the " Rose " filling in the " Lovers' Knot," " Butterfly " and " Fan " *motifs*, also an illustrated diagram showing all working details, will be found on pages 57 and 60.

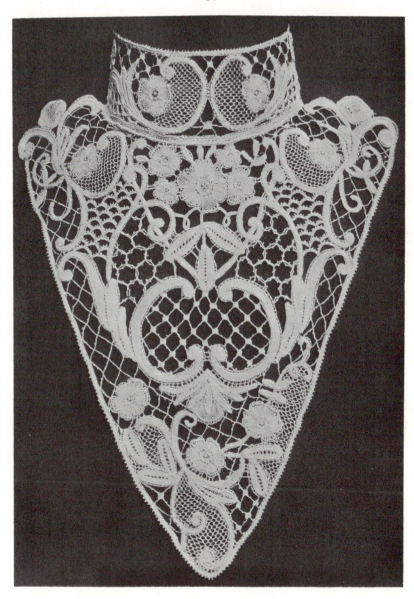

Vest in Guipure de Flandre.

## GUIPURE DE FLANDRE

We come now to one of the handsomest Guipure laces in existence, "Guipure de Flandre," a lace that is comparatively very little known or taught in England, although at the same time one of the most fascinating laces to manufacture on account of the variety of beautiful stitches or "fillings" introduced in this lace. The rich, heavy cord outline in this "Guipure de Flandre" differs also from the "Dentelle de Bruges" in the respect that it appears on the *right side of the lace only*, and has therefore a different movement.

As the little lace Vest offers such opportunity for learning a great variety of "Fillings," and makes such a wonderful piece of adornment, I should suggest starting on this. By the way, the little collar band is worked on a separate pattern and attached to the vest later.

Have ready six pairs of bobbins filled with No. 3 thread and one bobbin with Guipure cord, also a packet of *fine* lace pins, work the narrow braid first all round the vest, commencing at the top on two pins, work the ordinary

E

braid, with the straight open edge on the inside and open edge with " Picots " on the outer side using the Guipure cord as follows :—Thread the cord through the other bobbins into position, *and on working from right to left pass this cord through the last pair of bobbins but one, exactly the same as in the "Dentelle de Bruges," but on the return row, that is from left to right, simply work over the cord instead of passing it through the bobbins as usual;* repeat this all through. You will notice that *two* cords are used on all the scrolls (one each side), and *one* cord for the flowers and leaves, the flowers being worked exactly the same as in the Dentelle de Bruges except that every alternate petal is " Half" stitch. The cord is carried down to the ring of the flower and back again at the division of each petal in the same manner as in the Dentelle de Bruges; the large leaves are also worked exactly the same, whilst the smaller leaves are worked in plain " Cloth " stitch (like the braid) with the open edge each side, but no vein down the middle.

Eight pairs of bobbins are required for the larger flowers and leaves, six pairs being sufficient for the smaller flowers and leaves, whilst ten pairs are necessary for the large scrolls besides the two cords. The " Fillings " are put in separately at the finish, and comprise " Reseau," " Festoon," " Spider," " Honeycomb " and " Plait " stitches.

N.B.—A certain amount of skill is necessary to keep the form of the design in making lace, and particularly is this noticeable round the curves of the scrolls—commence these on three pins, placing the first pin at the bend on the inner line where the scroll curves completely round. Place the next pin in the centre of this little round curve and the last pin between the other two pins. Hang on your bobbins (a pair at a time) and work " Cloth " stitch right across, commencing at the inner pin, thread the cord (tied together on a pair of bobbins) through the other bobbins over one and under another, leaving it hanging each side in between the two last pairs, and work across every row to the middle of the scroll, using one cord only on the outer open edge of braid where the pins are placed, and working plain " Cloth " stitch on the inside without any open edge or pins, continue this all round ; when you reach the top, however, you should begin to connect the two inner sides together, continue to do this every row until you get quite round the curve and arrive opposite to the first pin, then take in the other cord, and work open edge each side for the straight portion of the scroll, and, if it *finishes in another round curve* as is often the case, then work this curve also in a circle as at the commencement.

## YOKE IN GUIPURE DE FLANDRE

This handsome Yoke is worked in similar style to the Vest, and the detailed instructions given for the latter will apply to this Yoke in the main.  Perhaps it would be as well to explain, however, that the large ornamental leaves at the outside points of the design are worked in three sections, the middle or inner section being worked as an ordinary " Bruges " leaf, in " Cloth " stitch with seven pairs of bobbins and one Guipure cord throwing out the vein of the leaf over a pin each time, as previously described.  The extreme outer section is next worked, adding an extra pair of bobbins, as also an extra cord ; the space between these two sections being filled in last with " Half" stitch, connecting every row, on each side, to the parts already worked.   The same " braid border" is worked round the smaller leaves, whilst the handsome "Double Reseau" filling is described on page 60.  The medallions are also worked in three sections, the inner and outer " braid " being worked first and the middle space last ; this is done in " Half " stitch

Yoke in Guipure de Flandre.

connecting each row to this worked " braid " as previously
described.  The little circles round the neck of the Yoke
are worked in " Cloth " stitch with two cords (one each
side) crossing these cords as described on page 25 at the
division of each circle, the ornamental line underneath the
circles is worked in " Stem " stitch with five pairs of bobbins
and one cord bobbin as follows:—Work the cord on the
*outer edge* of the stem, where also place the pins, making
the usual " open edge " on this side by twice twisting the two
outer pairs of bobbins before and after your last stitch, but
on the inner side of the stem *no pins are used, and the
twists must be omitted.*

## BOLERO IN GUIPURE DE FLANDRE

This handsome Bolero, which by the way is worked in No. 2 thread and a heavy Guipure cord, needs (after the Vest and Yoke) very little explanation. The very effective " Diamond " filling described on page 59 shows here to great advantage. The little open *dots* or *holes* that occur in some of the flowers and leaves are made as described on page 81, in the Antique Honiton scarf, except that *no pins are used here in making these openings.* The centres of the flowers are filled in with different " Needle " stitches, (see page 99).

Bolero in Guipure de Flandre.

52

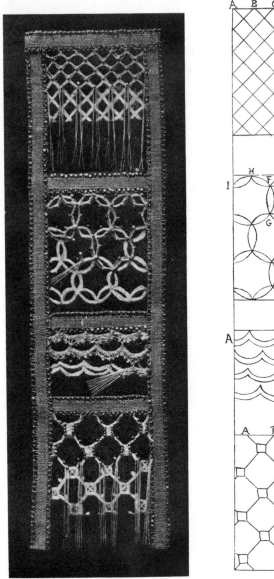

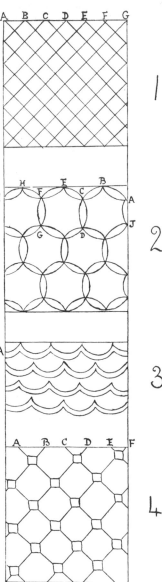

Ornamental Lace Stitches          Working diagram of the "Stitches."
"Reseau," "Honeycomb," "Festoon,"
and "Spider Web."

## ORNAMENTAL LACE STITCHES

### No. 1.   RESEAU

This " Reseau " stitch forms a handsome background to a great many different kinds of Lace, and is worked as follows :—Connect one pair of bobbins at A (No. 1 diagram) and two pairs at B, C, D, E and F, also one pair at G— twist the A pair twice to the left, also the nearest B pair, make a " Cloth " stitch with these two pairs, stick a pin on the cross between these bobbins and make another " Cloth " stitch round this pin, twisting each pair once to the left before making the stitch—drop these two pairs, and repeat with the next two, viz. the unworked B pair and the nearest C pair.  Continue until all the bobbins are worked, connect at the end of the row and return in the same manner—noting that *if the space you are filling increases in width, an extra pair of bobbins must be added at the end of each row ; whilst if it decreases, a pair must be cut off each time*—this of course refers to all " Fillings."

### No. 2.   HONEYCOMB

This very pretty " filling " is worked in " Plait " stitch (described on page 17). Connect two pairs of bobbins at A (No. 2 diagram).  " Plait " to B on the *top* line, making a " Picot " in the middle, place a pin at B and work a "Cloth" stitch round it.  Plait to C on the lower line and repeat, plait to point D and back again to C, work a second "Cloth" stitch round the pin at C, plait from C to E on the top line, then from E to F on the lower line. Now " Plait " from F to G and back again to F, working a second " Cloth " stitch round the pin at F, " Plait " to H on the top line, and H to I on the lower line, connect at point I to the lace and return on the remaining lines back to A, drawing the pins out at all the *lettered points* on this return row as you arrive at them, viz. H, F, E, C, and B, and connecting through the " Plait " here with the working bobbins. Continue the " Plait " to J, connect again here and work this row exactly the same as the last.

## No. 3.   " FESTOON "

This stitch, though remarkably easy, is most graceful and effective and is worked as follows :—Connect five pairs of bobbins at A and work " Cloth " stitch across to the lower line of the scallop, twisting the two last pairs twice before making the last stitch, add a Picot by twisting the outer pair three times, pin down, make another " Cloth " stitch, twist each pair twice again, and return with plain " Cloth " stitch to the top of the row, omitting the twists and not placing any pins here, work back again to the outer edge of the scallop, where repeat the open edge and Picot.

## No. 4. "SPIDER" WEB STITCH

One of the most popular "fillings" is the "Spider" web, partly from its adaptability to all sized spaces and partly from its bold distinctive appearance, which seems to supply a character and effect to all these laces. Connect two pairs of bobbins at A, same at B, C, D, E and F. "Plait" A bobbins across to the corner of the nearest little square and leave them (making a picot in the middle of the "strand" as you plait), do the same with B and leave them at the opposite corner of the same little square (to avoid the bobbins becoming entangled here, simply hang them over a pin at each corner). Repeat the directions just given with C and D bobbins for the next "Web" and E and F for the last "Web" on this row. Now return to A and B bobbins, remove the pins over which the bobbins are hanging and work "Cloth" stitch with all four pairs of bobbins from left to right, stick the pin back again in the right-hand corner, work a "Cloth" stitch round the pin and right across to the left-hand corner, place another pin here and repeat, continue to work "Cloth" stitch, placing pins at the end of each row as closely together as possible until the whole square is worked. "Plait" the strands across to the lower row, and leave them hanging whilst you work C and

D, also E and F. On the next row you will require two more pairs of bobbins connecting on at the first "Web" to work with A bobbins, B and C will work together in this row as D and E, whilst F will be connected to the lace and brought down at the back of the lace for the third row.

## No. 5.  "LEAD" FILLING

The next is the famous Honiton "lead" filling, one of the most difficult but at the same time one of the richest stitches in Lace-making, and the result is certainly well worth the time spent in acquiring the necessary knack and skill to accomplish this stitch successfully. Commence at the top of the space with two pairs of bobbins at A, twist each pair twice to the left, and weave with the outer right-hand bobbin over and under the other three bobbins until you nearly reach the cross, now drop these bobbins. Hang two pairs on at B and weave as with A bobbins until you arrive at the same cross. Now take the nearest pairs of A and B bobbins, work a "Cloth" stitch, place a pin in the upper dot and work another "Cloth" stitch round the pin, twist both pairs of bobbins twice, work a "Cloth" stitch, place a pin in the right-hand

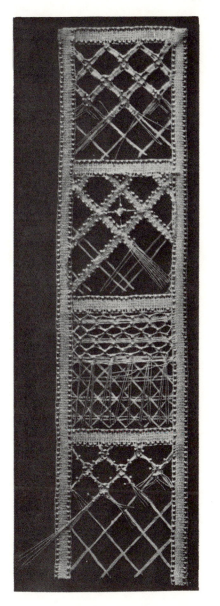

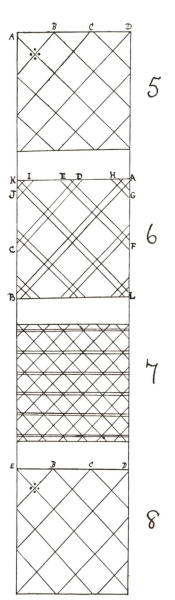

Ornamental Lace Stitches.
"Lead," "Diamond," "Double Reseau,"
and "Rose."

Working diagram of the "Stitches"

F

dot and work another " Cloth " stitch round this pin ; now do the same with A bobbins, placing the pin in the left-hand dot, and lastly twist the two nearest pairs of A and B, and work a " Cloth " stitch round a pin in the lower dot. Hang two more pairs of bobbins at B and two at C and repeat.

## No. 6. " DIAMOND " STITCH

This is a bold, handsome " filling " for large spaces. Connect five pairs of bobbins at A, work " Cloth " stitch across from left to right, stick a pin on the right-hand line, work a " Cloth " stitch round the pin. " Cloth " stitch across, placing a pin on the left-hand line, where also work a stitch round this pin, repeat until you reach B, where connect, wrap, and tie your bobbins together and continue them at the back of the lace which is the side you are working on (see illustration) until you reach C, connect here and work across to D, repeat the connection here, also at E, and work across to F, then from G to H, here the bobbins must be fastened off, cut close, and five fresh pairs connected at I, worked to J, connect again ; and again at K, working across to L, and so on until all the lines are worked.    Next fill in all the diamond spaces with the *woven* Spiders described on page 17.

## No. 7.   "DOUBLE  RESEAU"

This extremely elaborate stitch is really not so complicated to work as it appears, and is very uncommon. Commence as for ordinary "reseau" and follow the directions given for this stitch until you arrive at the first of the double parallel lines, connect an extra pair of bobbins here and work "Cloth" Stitch right across with these, taking in each of the hanging bobbins in turn and twisting the *working pair* twice each time in between.    Connect at the end of the row and return in exactly the same manner, bringing this extra pair of bobbins down at the end of the row to the next double line and leave them ready until you have worked the "reseau" in between.

## No. 8.   "ROSE" FILLING

This very lacey stitch is worked in a similar manner to the "lead" filling, except that the bars are plaited instead of woven, and consequently it is very much easier of execution.

Connect two pairs of bobbins at E and work " Plait " stitch to the middle of the strand, twist each of the outside threads round a separate pin and pin down to form a small picot each side, continue the plait until the cross is almost reached ; now hang two pairs of bobbins at B and do the same, working the cross with all four pairs, placing a pin in each dot as in the " lead " filling.

## HONITON

Amongst rare and valuable laces Honiton ranks very high, the finer specimens, particularly of "raised" Honiton (which in character bears a very close resemblance to Brussels) being equal to any Bobbin Lace in existence. Honiton Bobbin Lace may be divided into three branches, Honiton, Honiton *appliqué*, and "raised" Honiton. The little "Rose" Collar is a specimen of the first named, the "Foxglove" Border of the second, whilst the antique Scarf and *Flounce* combine the "raised" work and the *appliqué*.

These two valuable specimens, kindly lent me time and again by the owner for reproduction by my pupils, will I feel sure serve as an encouragement and incentive to my readers to strive to achieve what our ancestors accomplished so successfully in years gone by, and, with such beautiful models before them, aim at producing lace worthy of being likewise handed down to posterity.   Such examples as these form striking proof that at one time (if not at present) English-made lace could rival that of any other country in the world.

Now as the " raised " work requires greater skill and care than any other branch of Bobbin Lace it is necessary that the lace-maker has obtained a certain amount of proficiency before attempting this work, which, by the way, amongst professional lace-makers, is considered the highest and is consequently the best paid branch in Lace-making—for, as is the case in all branches of a craft requiring exceptional skill, experts are rare.

It may, perhaps, be as well at this point to give a general explanation of the term "raised" Honiton, which no doubt to several of my readers is very confusing. The lace really obtains its name from the raised cord bordering parts of the design, this cord being unlike any other, as it is made on the *pillow* by the worker as she proceeds, and thereby serves a double purpose ; for, apart from enriching the lace, the worker can by means of this cord proceed from one part of the design to another where she would otherwise be obliged to cut off the bobbins and re-start, and so is able to avoid more fastening off than would be possible otherwise ; a very desirable object in the making of fine lace.

## "ROSE" COLLAR IN HONITON

For working the little collar, commence with the large ornamental medallion.  Stick three pins in the top of the scroll where it curves round, and hang on nine pairs of bobbins filled with No. 3 lace thread and one pair filled with Honiton Gimp (which differs from the Bruges cord in that it is flat rather than round), the gimps must be placed in exactly the same position as the cord in the Bruges lace (i.e. in between the two outer pairs of bobbins at each side).  Do not pass this cord as before, however, but simply *work it as an ordinary bobbin in "Cloth" stitch* with the others, taking care that it always remains in the two exact positions assigned to it, viz. on working across from right to left after working the left-hand gimp (previous to making your twisted outer edge and putting in the pin on this side) the gimp will be between the second and third pairs of bobbins ; as soon, however, as you work it again on the return row it will be between the first and second pairs of bobbins—the same also with the right-hand gimp

65

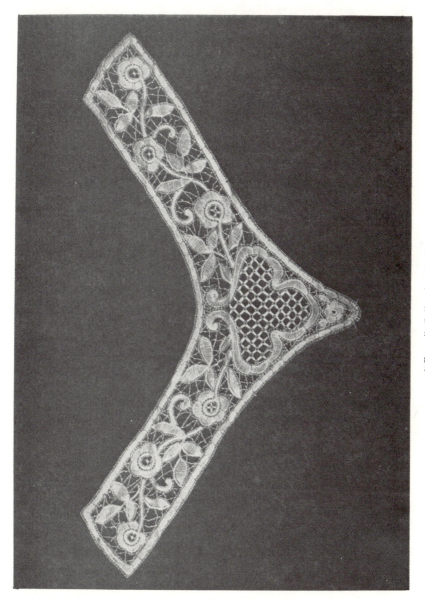

" Rose " Collar in Honiton.

Work round the scroll in the same way as described in Guipure de Flandre, page 43, but taking in *both gimps*, though neither twisting the bobbins nor placing any pins on the inner side, until you are quite round the curve, remembering also to connect the lace in the middle of the curve as many times as necessary.

However, as soon as you are round the scroll, work the ordinary "open edge" each side of the braid, and continue as usual until you reach the first scollop where the outer edge of the medallion curves inwards ; at this point (*on the return row from left to right*) twist each of your outer two pairs of bobbins twice as usual, take the left-hand gimp *under* all the other fourteen bobbins *over* the right-hand gimp, and back again, then work this gimp as usual. Repeat this at every scollop or wherever the curve inclines inwards. The stem of one of the flowers on either side of this medallion should be worked next ; for this connect five pairs of bobbins and one pair of gimp into the lace already worked.

Make ordinary braid for the stem and ring of the flower, connect the ring together and continue the petals in cloth stitch, making the same open edge round the outside of the petals and working "Cloth" Stitch only without any twists on the inside (using the inner gimp as before in the scroll) and connecting every row to the ring—before commencing these petals it will be necessary to connect two extra pairs of bobbins to the ring.

To commence the leaf at the top of the group on the upper side of the stem stick two pins quite close together at the tip of the leaf and work " Cloth " stitch across with six pairs of bobbins, thread the gimp (one pair) over and under these bobbins until in the right position (one each side), stick a pin at either side of the leaf close to the top in *front* of the two last pairs, twist each pair twice, drop the outer pair, work " Cloth " stitch with the inner pair, taking up a gimp and a thread bobbin for the first stitch, and work across in plain " Cloth " stitch, these leaves having no vein in the middle.

Make the ordinary " open edge " as usual each side and add an extra pair of bobbins as required. When you reach the stem cut off the gimps and any extra bobbins you may have added (tying these latter securely together in pairs, before cutting off) and work the little stem with five pairs of bobbins, making the " open edge " and placing the pins on the *outer edge of the stem only* whilst the inner side is worked in plain " Cloth " stitch without any pins. This " Stem " stitch, which is used for all fine stems, is invariably worked in this manner and always with five (or six) pairs of bobbins. Connect at the finish to the stem of the flower, taking the bobbins across to the other side of this stem, connect again there and continue to work the leaf, adding on an extra pair of bobbins where required, as before; the two leaves belonging to the upper groups are worked in the same manner, commencing at the tip of one and finishing at the tip of the other.

The braid round the edge of the collar is worked with nine pairs of bobbins and one pair of gimps. Work as for ordinary braid, but at every fifth pin cross the right-hand gimp into the place of the left-hand gimp and this latter into the place of the right-hand gimp and proceed as before. The " Plaited " Strands are the same as in the Dentelle de Bruges except that the Honiton workers are rather more lavish with the " Picots." For the beautiful Honiton stitch in the centre medallion—appropriately named by the workers "lead" filling on account of its resemblance to the lead work in stained and ornamental window panes—you will require a great many bobbins, which should be wound and tied up ready in pairs.

Full directions for working this stitch, with illustrated diagram showing all details, are given on page 56.

## "FOXGLOVE" BORDER IN HONITON
## *APPLIQUÉ*

The lower part of this very handsome design is worked
first on the cushion, next the narrow little upper ornament,
and, lastly, the braid.  When all the lace is completely
finished, ready to be appliquéd on the net (which, by the
way, should be real Brussels), cut a strip of net the length
required, eight inches in width.   Have ready the complete
working design (pinned down on the cushion as usual), lay
one end of the net over this, now take your finished lace and
pin it carefully down on top on the net (over the pattern)
using the fine lace pins ; when ready fixed in position, thread
a fine needle with No. 4 lace thread, and neatly attach the
extreme edge of the lace to the net—the net is afterwards
cut away from behind the open parts with special ball-
pointed scissors—before doing this, however, it is advisable
to work in the little dots powdered over the upper portion
of the net, these are put in with the needle and No. 2
thread *after the lace is removed from the cushion*, and are
made with four chain stitches, one on each strand of the mesh

71

"Foxglove" Border or Flounce (8½ inches deep) in Honiton *Applique*.

of the net, leaving an open diamond in the middle. Commence on the right side of the net with a long end of thread which afterwards cut close and finish by running through the last stitch at the back. These little circles are very quickly worked and greatly enrich the net.

The working of the lace itself will be quite clear from the illustration, two gimps being used in every part of the design except the stems, and for these five pairs of bobbins only are used without gimps.

For the braid at the top of the lace hang on eight pairs of bobbins only (no gimps), work " Cloth " stitch across with the four right-hand pairs, twisting the two outer pairs twice before sticking in the pin and making the stitch at the back of the pin as usual, work back again with the same four pairs and stick a pin on the inner right-hand line in between the two last pairs of bobbins and work a " Cloth " stitch round the pin without twists. Now work back again with the same bobbins to the outer edge and return once more to the inner edge, stick a pin in between the last two pairs on this side ; do not work a " Cloth " stitch round this pin, however, but simply leave the bobbins hanging. Work exactly the same with the four left-hand pairs of bobbins, sticking the pins on the left-hand lines of the braid, and when you arrive at exactly opposite the same point where you left off on the

G

other side, proceed to make the first woven bars in the middle of the braid which is done as follows :—

Twist your inner pair of bobbins on the left-hand side once, take the outer bobbin of this pair across and *over* the inner pair on the right-hand side, bring it back *under* the same pair, also *over* and *under* the odd bobbin on the left-hand side—repeat this six times, finishing on the left-hand side ; tie this pair together, work a " Cloth " stitch with the next pair round the pin already in, and proceed as at the beginning.

76

Copy of Old Honiton Scarf in "raised" work and *Appliqué*.

For pattern of central spray see folding sheet 2.

## " RAISED " HONITON

The next attempt is to be a copy of the antique Lace Scarf which, by the way, makes an exquisite Veil for a bride as well as a priceless dress ornamentation. The detail of the scarf (the work of one of my pupils) is shown on page 79, ready to be appliquéd on the net. This scarf is worked in No. 4 thread, a gimp being used on each side of the stems and the flowers ; the leaves being all edged with the " raised " cord, no gimp is necessary for these.

The lace-maker will by this time have learnt to gauge the number of bobbins required for different portions of the designs in the various sized threads for herself.

It will be best to begin on one of the little " Border " designs of the scarf. Commence to make the " raised " cord on the edge of the leaves, which is made with five pairs of bobbins, choose the branch with the five little leaves and commence at the foot of the top leaf on two pins set very close together ; work as for the narrow stems having the open edge pinned down, each row on the outer side of the leaf, and work the inner in the following manner :—" Cloth " stitch with all except the last inner pair, now cross the *working* pair once to the left, throw it out and work back with the *next* pair, taking care that it is also *crossed once to the left, for the first " Cloth " stitch ;* repeat this every row. When you arrive at the extreme tip of the leaf (note the cord is made on *one* side of the leaves only) proceed to work the leaf itself by " Cloth " stitching across to the opposite side of the leaf, making the ordinary open edge here and placing the pins as usual.    " Cloth" stitch back again to the cord just made, draw out the top pin of this and connect the leaf you are working to this cord by simply inserting a crochet hook in the place where the pin has been, and drawing the nearest bobbin through as previously described; work " Cloth " stitch across to the other side—open edge— pin, and return with " Cloth " stitch right up to the cord, *as no open edge is made now on the cord side of the leaf*, take out the next pin in the cord and attach a new pair of bobbins in the place where this pin has been ; work " Cloth " stitch across with this new pair, repeat this for the next two rows or until you have added three extra pairs of bobbins ; at the finish of the leaf these extra bobbins must be tied together in pairs (making three tight knots,

Showing the large ornamental spray on the Scarf worked ready for
appliquing on to the net.

For full-size pattern see folding sheet 2.

reversing the tie each time) and cut off close. Continue to work the "raised" cord down the stem with the remaining five pairs of bobbins until you arrive at the next leaf on the stem, continue the cord then up the lower edge of this leaf to the extreme tip and work the leaf as before. When this is completed, work the opposite leaf in the same manner, then work the little portion of stem in between this and the next leaf and so on to the end, connecting the stem each time you cross over it—the few remaining leaves are worked in the same manner, whilst for the flowers and buds two gimps are used and no "raised" cord. The "Brick" filling in the middle of the large flower is worked exactly the same as the "Lead" filling, with the exception that *no "Cloth" stitches are made in between the woven bars.* After the first row of woven bars are made, take two bobbins from one bar, and the two nearest bobbins from the next bar, twist each pair twice, weave another bar, and repeat to the end of the row.

After you have finished the Border of the Scarf, proceed to work the large ornamental Spray in the same manner, using two gimps for all the flowers, buds and stems, and making the "raised" cord in the leaves. The leaves with the slits or openings in the middle—a style much favoured in antique lace—are made by working half way across the leaf only (until you come to the mark indicated on your pattern), then work a " Cloth " stitch round a pin, return to the outer edge of the leaf and back again six times, or until you have worked three pins in the middle—now drop these bobbins and work the other side of the leaf with the other half of the bobbins (remembering to work these leaves with an even number of bobbins) ; for the seventh row work across as usual and continue until you come to the next opening.

Perhaps one of the most ornamental variety of leaves is that with the open vein of " Woven " Bars up the middle, and though these leaves are rather more complicated to work, they well repay the lace-maker for the extra trouble by the richness and beauty of the effect.   Commence with the stem of the leaf, working this in the ordinary way, i.e. plain "Cloth" stitch on the inner side and pinning down the outer side with its open edge.   Continue this right up to the top of the inside of the leaf (as indicated by the traced pattern), work round and down the other side until you come to the line indicating the first bar ; now take the nearest pair of bobbins across this line and connect through the inner " Cloth " stitch on the other side of the leaf, bring the same pair of bobbins back again, threading them over and under the next pair of bobbins, now take them across again, and again connect in the same place, repeat this once more,

Showing part of the Border of the Scarf worked ready for appliquing
on to the net.

and on bringing them back to their right place work an extra "Cloth" stitch round the pin to prevent the bar slipping.

When you have finished this portion of the leaf, commence to work the "raised" cord (with the same five pairs of bobbins) up the lower edge of the first division of the leaf, remembering to twist your inner bobbins for this cord as explained previously, each of these little divisions of the leaf are edged with the "raised" cord and worked exactly like the little separate leaves—connecting them to the middle portion of the leaf and also to each other where necessary.

After working one half of the leaf, *including the topmost part*, the bobbins should be tied up and cut off, commencing again at the lowest division to work the other half.

## ANTIQUE HONITON FLOUNCE

### (Lilies of the Valley, Forget-me-nots, Jessamine, Wild Rose and Convolvulus Design.)

This exquisite Flounce with its wealth of beautiful Wild Flowers is executed almost entirely in "Cloth" stitch with the Cord edge, the filling in the Convolvulus being done in "Brick" stitch, whilst the lower part of this flower has a trellis of woven bars. The Forget-me-nots have two petals of each flower worked in "Cloth" stitch, the three remaining petals being worked in the "Stem" stitch which (as previously described) is worked with five pairs of bobbins having the "Open edge" and pins on the outer side only.

Copy of very valuable Old Honiton Flounce

("Lilies of the Valley," "Forget-me-nots," "Jessamine," "Wild Rose," and "Convolvulus.")

For full-size pattern see folding sheet 1.

## DUCHESSE

Another exquisite lace is " Duchesse," which though somewhat resembling the Dentelle de Bruges is a type of Lace that calls for an altogether finer and more elaborate treatment, and consequently admits of a greater beauty of design than the latter. The Lace Edge (that we are about to work) illustrates this, and one can understand that to connoisseurs and lovers of valuable lace, Duchesse is very dearly prized.

It must be understood that in working this Lace the Cord has the same movement as in the Dentelle de Bruges, and must not be confused with the Honiton.

The illustrated specimen was worked in No. 4 lace thread with cord to match, and the "fine" pins. To commence the pattern, place three pins at the top of the basket (for the row of ornamental circles in " Half" stitch), work seven pairs of bobbins across in " Cloth " stitch, thread a pair of cord bobbins through into position, and work these circles exactly the same as described on page 25 in the Doyley, following the directions given there. When you arrive at the end of

H

this row of circles, cut off one cord, wrap and tie the remaining cord and the thread bobbin as described on page 38,
until they reach the next line of the basket (indicated
on the working pattern) and work this row in " Cloth " stitch,
connecting each row to the circles and working plain
" Cloth " stitch right up to the connections, whilst the cord is
worked on the opposite side (where the pins are placed)
working the ordinary twisted " open edge " here.

All the bobbins and cord are again tied together at the end
of the row (connecting to the lace if necessary) until they
reach the next line, and so on until the entire basket is
worked, throwing out the " Woven bars " in the very last row,
which are done in exactly the same manner as those in the
large leaves on the Honiton scarf, the working details being
given on page 82. The handle of the basket is worked
the same as the first row, whilst the little flowers are worked
in " Cloth " stitch, using five pairs of bobbins and a single cord
for the centre ring, pinning down the outer edge of the ring
only, with a twisted " open edge " on this side only. The
roses are worked in sections of " Cloth " stitch and " Half "
stitch — the buds and the leaves having the " Woven
bars " up the middle, the latter are worked *up* one side
first in " Half " stitch, and *down* the other side in " Cloth "
stitch, throwing out the " Bars " as indicated on the pattern.

Lace Border in "Duchesse." (4 inches deep.)
"Baskets of Flowers" and "Ribbon" design.

For full-size pattern see folding sheet 2.

You will require nine pairs of bobbins and one cord for the " ribbon " which is connected down the middle to form an open vein. To do this, work plain " Cloth " stitch up to the line indicated on the pattern, place a pin on this line, each time, and work a " Cloth " stitch round the pin, *first twisting your outer pair of bobbins twice to the left*. When the whole length of the " ribbon " is worked, connect at each of these pins as you arrive at them by twisting the nearest pair of bobbins once to the left *before* you draw the thread through, and also twisting once again *after* the thread is drawn through. The braid at the top of the Lace is described on page 73, whilst the " Strands " are " Plaited " across with two pairs of bobbins making two " Picots " in each division (where indicated on the pattern) connecting the return row of " strands " right through the " Plait " as they cross.

## BRUSSELS

The last species in the book and at the same time perhaps the most renowned of all Bobbin Lace is Brussels ; this consists of two varieties, the first being simply known as " Brussels," and the second as " Brussels *appliqué*" (by the way, the latter must not be confounded with Brussels Point de Gaze, a lace also of exceptional beauty, but entirely made with the needle and consequently far more tedious and trying to manufacture than the Bobbin variety).

In *all* Brussels lace, however, a little inlet of Needle-made stitches occur in special portions of the design, which not only distinguishes it from any other species of Bobbin Lace, but also adds an especial beauty and character peculiar to Brussels Lace. This is particularly noticeable in the examples given. Take for instance the " Lilac" collar with its large medallions enriched with handsome " Needle" lace stitches as also a few of the leaves—the mass of the work being Bobbin-made. Then again the " Peacock feather" handkerchief with its little inlet of Needle lace in the corner and sides only ; and lastly the *Berthè* in Brussels

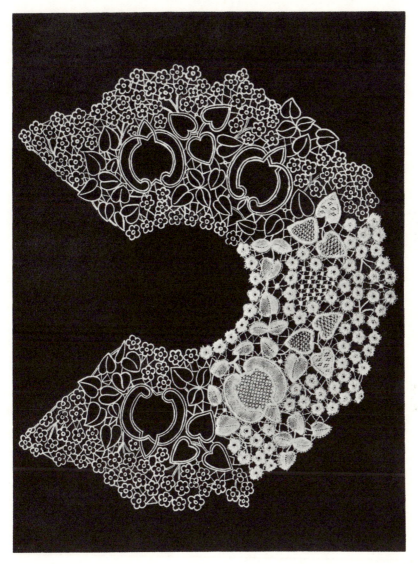

Collar in Brussels Lace. " Lilac "

*appliqué* where the *Needle* and Bobbin-made stitches are intermingled in the Buttercups and Daisies with such a beautiful result.

All the illustrated specimens are worked in No. 4 thread, whilst for the *Needle* stitches No. 3 is used. In working the Collar, commence with the flowers, using five pairs of bobbins for the little ring; placing the pins and working the " open edge " on the outside only ; after completing the ring, attach one cord and one extra pair of bobbins for the petals which are worked entirely in " Cloth " stitch in the usual way, remembering to add "Picots " on those flowers bordering the design ; at the finish of each flower cut off the cord, also tie and cut off the extra pair of bobbins. Now buttonhole the other five pairs (with one of the number) closely together for six times, reach the threads across to the ring of the next nearest blossom, buttonhole them again six times, pin down through this to the ring you are about to work, and when finished cut away the threads (reaching from one blossom to another,) close to the buttonholed portions and pin these back behind the flower on the wrong side of lace.

From seven to ten pairs of bobbins and one cord are required for working the leaves according to their size ; these are done in "Cloth" stitch on the one side, throwing out the " vein " on a pin each time as described on page 24 and the other side in " Half " stitch, remembering also for these to add "Picots" where indicated.   For the " braid " edge round the " Needle-filled " leaves, five pairs of bobbins and one pair of cords are used, whilst for the stems five pairs are used *without* the cords.   The same " braid " edge is also worked round the large medallion with five pairs of bobbins and one pair of cords, the space between this braid being afterwards filled in with " Half" stitch (for which four extra pairs of bobbins are required).   Commence the braid near the top of the medallion, and on completing this, and joining neatly together, cut off the two cords; wrapping up and tying the other bobbins together, connecting each tie to the braid, until they reach the extreme top of the medallion, work the little piece of braid going across to the other side, and then connect these five pairs to the edge of the braid inside the top of the medallion, add also two extra pairs of bobbins and work across in " Half" stitch, connect, work back to the other side, connect here by drawing a *new pair of bobbins* through the braid, and work across to the other side, where repeat.   You will now have nine pairs of bobbins ; continue working with these until the whole space between the " braids " is filled in with " Half" stitch, remembering to connect every row at each end to the braid. The large centre of the medallions are filled in with Needle Lace stitches.

All the "Strands" are bobbin-made, as also the "Spider Web" "filling" in the middle of the back of the Collar; directions for working this being given on page 55. To put in the *Needle* stitches (after the rest of the collar has been worked and taken off the cushion), baste the edge of the parts that require the "fillings" to a small piece of coloured glazed linen or American leather and proceed to work in any suitable lace stitches. The special stitches used on these specimens were taken from my book, "The New Lace Embroidery" (Punto Tagliato), which abounds in beautiful original stitches, for although this *new Punto Tagliato embroidery* is done in coarse silks, all the stitches are suitable for reproducing in fine threads.

You can, however, substitute any Needle Lace stitches you know, and the greater variety (provided they are suitable) the better the effect.

## HANDKERCHIEF IN BRUSSELS LACE

A great deal of the "*raised*" cord enters into the Brussels " Peacock feather " handkerchief, which, however, is made differently to the " *raised* " cord on the Honiton scarf, being for the greater part " tied " instead of " worked." Commence on the line indicated on your working pattern up the middle of one of the "feathers" with six pairs of bobbins, and work the cord exactly in the same way as described on page 77 for the Honiton scarf. Continue this quite round the tip and then work the first little divison (indicated in the design) exactly the same as a leaf, adding two extra pairs of bobbins ; when this is completed, proceed to make the "*raised*" cord up the next little division with the whole eight pairs of bobbins as follows—Lay the middle fourteen bobbins together on the cushion, with the outer bobbin (of each side) apart ; now take the right-hand bobbin, pass it carefully *under* these fourteen bobbins and *over* the *left-hand bobbin*, bringing this latter back in the same way, now cross the right-hand bobbin over the top of all the other and repeat with the left-hand bobbin—pull both outer bobbins tight so that the others are twisted into a thick cord ; continue this until you almost reach the top of the leaf, when leave out one pair of bobbins (do not cut these off, however). When

Handkerchief in Brussels Lace.

" Peacock Feather " design.

you reach the top leave out a second pair, work round the tip in the " worked " *raised* cord as at the commencement— now work this second division of the " feather " exactly the same as the first, taking in the two pairs of bobbins (dropped out of the cord as you arrive at them—by the way, this cord should be pinned down to the pattern at intervals as you make it, pinning right through the middle of the cord ; and in connecting insert the crochet hook through the *wrapping threads* only. Continue to make the " tied " cord at every section now, finishing the extreme tip with the " worked " cord, and when the left-hand side of the " feather " is finished fasten off all the bobbins and commence at the top to work the next half. The whole of the " braid " portion of the design is worked with five pairs of bobbins and a pair of cords, the braid at the extreme edge of the handkerchief being worked in one piece by being carried at the back of the ornamental border (which must be worked first), using seven pairs of bobbins and one cord. The " Woven bars " in the " feathers " are put in separately with two pairs of bobbins, weaving over and under the other three bobbins six times, then connected through the braid, after which tie this right-hand pair together once, and twist on to the next Bar, when, before commencing to weave, connect again through the lace and tie — connecting and tying the left-hand pair in the same way.

## BERTHÈ IN BRUSSELS *APPLIQUÉ*

The " Buttercup and Daisy" Berthè in Brussels *appliqué*
is made in separate sections on the cushion, and afterwards
appliquéd to the net.  Six pairs of bobbins and one cord
are used for the " braid " edge of the buttercups, working
the " open edge " each side of the " braid " and the
" Picots " as indicated on the pattern ; the middle of the
flower is worked in five pairs (without the cord) with the
" open edge " and pins on the outer side only—this part
(as indicated by the pattern) is worked in one set of
bobbins without leaving off.  Two pairs of bobbins are
left hanging for the " Spider Web " at the finish, and an
extra four pairs added at the lines indicated on the pattern,
the " Spider Web " being worked as described on page 29.

The stitches in the petals are Needle-made, and must
be put in (as for the Collar, &c.), after the Bobbin-made
sections are complete.  Seven pairs and one cord are used
for the daisies, working the ring as for ordinary braid and
the petals in Cloth stitch with an open vein up the middle
—the braid round the edge of the Berthè is also worked
with this vein up the middle.  The leaves are the same,
except that one side is worked in " Cloth " and the other
in " Half " stitch, whilst the little grasses are worked in

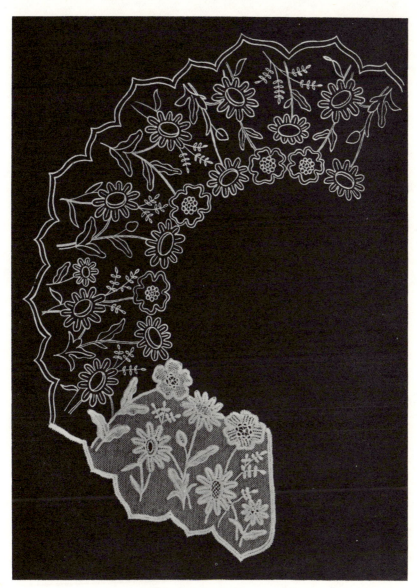

*Berthè* in Brussels *Appliqué.*   (7 inches deep.)

" Buttercups and Daisies."                              I

the "raised" cord. As each section of lace is completed it can be taken off the cushion and the *needle* stitches put in as described on page 99. I should suggest a different Lace stitch being used in every Buttercup for one half of the *Berthè* and repeated on the other half. A great variety of stitches can also be used with charming effect in the centres of the Daisies.

As each section of Lace is completed, it is best to lay them carefully in folds of paper until all are finished. The "braid" along the outer edge of the Berthè should be worked the last in one continuous piece.

To mount the Lace, cut a piece of Brussels net the size of the Berthè, lay it on your cushion over the design, pin down into position and sew the sections of lace to the net as described on page 70.

If the reader has carefully followed me through this book, and reproduced the greater part of the specimens illustrated, she will by now have acquired a collection of rare and valuable lace, for all time—whilst the knowledge and interest of having made it herself will greatly add to the enjoyment of possessing such lace, and the proud distinction of wearing it.

LOUISA A. TEBBS.

## HOW TO REPAIR BOBBIN LACE

The parts of the Lace that are torn or damaged must be replaced by new ones previously worked on the cushion, taking care to match the size of the thread, also the exact tint, which in the case of old lace is very difficult, and is best obtained by soaking white thread in weak tea or coffee (carefully strained through clean white blotting paper) until the exact tint is obtained.

Carefully sketch the little parts that you wish to work on coloured paper, taking for your model any that may be entire in the Lace, and work them in exactly the same stitches as the rest of the Lace is worked. When all are completed, cut out the damaged pieces from the Lace you are repairing and place the Lace on your cushion, fit your new little pieces into the places for which they are intended, pinning the edges down of both, all around the place you are repairing, and connect the "*old*" to the "*new*" parts very carefully with " Strands " made with two or four bobbins as required to match the rest of the lace.

These directions apply to all branches of Sectional Lace, but if the lace happens to be *appliquéd* on net, and there are torn or damaged places in the latter, this must also be carefully matched with new net and tinted if required in the same manner as the thread. In this case lay the torn pieces of net on stiff glazed coloured paper, tack it firmly to this paper, (taking the stitches about half an inch distant from the torn or jagged edge,) now cut a new piece of net rather larger than the damaged part you wish to repair, lay it over this damaged piece and tack it also firmly down to the paper, taking the stitches a quarter of an inch further in than the last. Thread a fine needle with No. 4 (or finer) lace thread and sew the two meshes of the net together all round (in between the tacking threads), then cut and trim the edges of both the " *old* " and " *new* " piece of net very carefully with ball-pointed scissors.

## HOW TO CLEAN VALUABLE LACE

Squeeze the Lace gently in warm soapy water made by stirring a small quantity of finely shredded good neutral soap into boiling water, stir until it is quite dissolved and forms a lather, allow the water to cool, dip the lace in and continue to squeeze it gently in the hand until quite clean— rinse in several changes of cold water, adding a little borax to the last water (in the proportion of a teaspoonful to a pint). Roll up the lace in a clean towel and press the towel a few times with the hand to get rid of the superfluous moisture; when this is done, take the lace out of the towel and pin it carefully down on a board large enough to take the entire piece.

This board must, however, be covered with a double thickness of white flannel over which is laid a clean white cloth (linen or cotton). Great care must be taken in pinning down the lace, which should be stretched securely in position with fine lace pins.

A certain amount of patience is necessary for this *very important part* of cleaning valuable lace, *the whole outline of the lace should be pinned down, including every little "Picot" both on the outside of the lace and on the "Strands."* If properly done, the lace will look as if it were just made, and will show no signs of having been washed. On the Continent (where all the valuable laces are cleaned in this manner) Lace-cleaning is a source of occupation gladly welcomed by reduced gentlewomen, who can follow it at their homes and add a considerable amount to their straitened incomes.

If the Lace is not very fine or of sufficient value to repay for all the time and trouble spent in pinning down, then a very good plan is to iron it on a board prepared as above, ironing the lace on the wrong side, and first laying a piece of white tissue paper between the Lace and the iron.

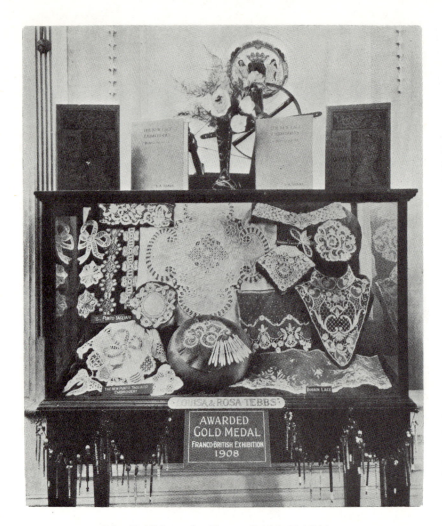

Prize Exhibit at the Franco-British Exhibition.

# SUPPLEMENT

TO

# THE ART OF BOBBIN LACE

## A Practical Text Book of Workmanship in Antique and Modern Bobbin Laces

INCLUDING

*VENETIAN, MILANESE, GENOESE, GUIPURE, FLEMISH, HONITON, DUCHESSE, AND BRUSSELS; ALSO SEVERAL RARE STITCHES AND FILLINGS FOR VARIOUS LACES*

WITH 38 ILLUSTRATIONS

BY

## LOUISA & ROSA TEBBS
*GOLD MEDALLISTS*

AUTHORS OF "THE NEW PUNTO TAGLIATO EMBROIDERY," AND PRINCIPALS
OF THE SCHOOL OF BOBBIN LACE EMBROIDERY AND DESIGN
14, UPPER BAKER STREET, LONDON, N.W.

Facsimile Edition
TO WHICH ARE ADDED RECENTLY
DISCOVERED PATTERNS PREPARED
BY THE AUTHOR

COMBINED ONE VOLUME EDITION
PUBLISHED BY
PAUL P. B. MINET
SACKVILLE STREET, LONDON, W.1.
1978

Reprinted in 1978 by
Paul P. B. Minet, Piccadilly Rare Books Ltd.,
30 Sackville Street, London,W1X 1DB


Originally published in 1911 by
Chapman and Hall Ltd., London




SBN  85609  030  1

*Printed in Great Britain by*
The Scolar Press Limited, Ilkley, Yorkshire

# PREFACE

THE demand and appreciation of "The Art of Bobbin Lace" since it first appeared has been so great that, in answer to the numerous and constant requests we have received from all parts of the world for an additional volume, we have decided to publish this Supplement in conjunction with the third edition of "The Art of Bobbin Lace," which is now ready.

To meet the needs of all those who have felt desirous of widening their knowledge of Lace-making beyond the first volume, we have given in this Supplement a collection of exquisite novelties in various Bobbin Laces (Antique and Modern) suitable for advanced pupils of the craft.

The thirty-eight specimens illustrated, which introduce many rare and beautiful stitches, include a Fan, Opera Bag, pair of Baby's Shoes, Table Centre and Afternoon Tea Cloth, D'Oyley, Yoke, Cravat, Motifs, Collars of various shapes (Peter Pan, Vandyke, Revers, Puritan, &c.), also several Edgings, Insertions and Flounces.

That the ancient craft of Bobbin Lace-making is now the acknowledged fashionable hobby, outrivalling even Bridge, is not to be wondered at, for it is not only the most fascinating of all Art Crafts, but it can be learned without difficulty and *at any age*.

Apart from the great value of the lace, a knowledge of Lace-making is an important and very interesting education in itself, enabling the expert not only to detect imitation lace at a glance, but also to distinguish all the different varieties of real lace, and to judge the *quality*—a very important knowledge when purchasing hand-made laces.

Many people have in the past been deterred from Lace-making under the impression that it is a strain on the eyes; this is a great mistake, however. Bobbin Lace-making is not in the least trying to the eyes; there is no work less so, even knitting, Bobbin Lace being made entirely by a series of weaving and plaiting movements with the bobbins, which in a very short time becomes almost mechanical, and it is a well-known fact that the professional lace-makers on the Continent rarely have occasion to wear spectacles even in old age.

It may serve as an encouragement to those who contemplate learning this craft to mention that at a recent exhibition of our pupils' work, which included a Lace

Dress, several long Scarves, Berthès, Fichus, Collars, Handkerchiefs, Vests, Boleros, Edgings, Insertions, and Flounces in every variety of species, the lace was not only remarkable for the quantity, but also for the exquisite finish and style, which was in the majority of cases quite professional, and had the work been for sale the whole of it would have readily found customers.

Several of our Colonial pupils have already started Lace industries in the Colonies to encourage thrifty workers, and with great success. The demand for hand-made lace was never greater than at present, and the secret of success in these industries, as we have repeatedly explained, is to maintain a very high standard, so that only first-class work is turned out, perfect in all the little details that so readily distinguishes professional from amateur work, and also to produce every variety of lace to suit all tastes and purposes.

It will be easily understood that sometimes one special lace is in favour, sometimes another. Again, some laces are more suitable for certain purposes than others, so that a substitute is not always advisable.

If the younger generation of our English Lace-makers (who are equal to any) were taught to make the different species of lace amongst them, instead of whole villages confining themselves to one special kind, they would not fail for lack of orders which are now executed abroad.

In conclusion, we would impress upon all Lace-makers the necessity of working only upon a perfectly accurately prepared Pattern—otherwise the lace is a hopeless failure. Those who have a task for designing or adapting their own patterns should first study the different branches of lace, as only a lace expert can prepare perfect working designs.

There are so many details to be noted in Lace-making that we find the Patterns require more careful and skilful drawing than for almost any other craft, and the value of the lace depends greatly on this.

Pricked Patterns, as we mentioned in the first volume of this book, should be strictly avoided for all these sectional varieties of Lace.

# CONTENTS

*b*

# LIST OF ILLUSTRATIONS *

*\* Several original patterns have been added to this edition, reproduced on two folding sheets at the back. They correspond to illustrations marked by an asterisk.*

Pagination of this Supplement is carried on from that of the main volume, The Art of Bobbin Lace, by L. A. Tebbs, originally published in 1908, and reprinted by us in 1972.

Peter Pan Collar, Lace Edging and D'Oyley in Venetian Lace ; also Flounce in Old Flemish.

## VENETIAN LACE

The Venetian Bobbin Lace, though without doubt one of the most beautiful of all laces, is certainly very difficult, and should not be attempted by a beginner. It is worked over a cord on one side of the lace. This cord, which gives a firm outline to the lace, is made with two pairs of bobbins filled with the same thread as used for making the lace. The Strands or Bars are thrown out as the lace is worked, not put in afterwards as in some of the laces.

" Venetian " stitch is always substituted for " Half " stitch in this lace, the petals of the flowers being worked alternately in " Venetian " stitch and " Cloth " stitch ; the stems are done entirely in the latter, whilst the small leaves are worked in " Venetian " stitch.

Three specimens of Venetian Lace are illustrated, viz., a Peter Pan Collar (3 inches deep), a Lace Edging (2½ inches wide), also a D'Oyley (8 inches across). All this Venetian Lace is worked in size 2 thread. We give the following directions for working the Collar, which also applies to the Lace Edging and D'Oyley. Commence working the flower by tying 4 bobbins and pin down at a little distance from the ring. Leave these and have ready 8 pairs of bobbins, stick 6 pins up the side of first petal commencing with the ring. Hang 1 pair of bobbins on each pin and 2 on the last pin, take the tied bobbins in the right hand and slip the remaining pair of bobbins on to these. Stick a pin in front of the last pin in the ring and work " Cloth " stitch through all the 7 pairs, twist both the last pairs twice, stick pin at the top of petal close to the other pin, twist each pair of passives once to the left, *work " Cloth " stitch and an extra twist with the inner pair down to the ring, pass the working pair under and over the tied bobbins, stick pin in front and leave. Start with the 2nd pair of bobbins from the top. " Cloth " stitch with 3rd pair, twist right-hand pair once, left-hand pair twice, stick pin at the top of the petal, " Cloth " stitch, twist both pairs twice ; start with the 2nd pair and work " Cloth " stitch and an extra twist down to the ring, passing the working pair under and over the tied pairs, stick pin in front, leave. Commence with 2nd and 3rd pairs at the top of the petal, " Cloth " stitch, twist right-hand pair once, the left-hand pair twice, stick pin at the top of the petal " Cloth " stitch behind pin. Twisting both pairs twice, work "Cloth" stitch and an extra twist with the 2nd pair down to the ring and leave. Repeat this a second time through 5 pairs, repeat a third time through 4 pairs, repeat again through 3 pairs and again through 2 pairs, "Cloth" stitch with the 2nd and 3rd pair at the top of the petal. Twist the right-hand pair once and the left-hand pair twice, stick pin at the top division of the petal and work "Cloth" stitch at the back of the pin, twisting both pairs twice leave the outer pair. Work "Cloth" stitch with the inner pair through all the others, pass this pair under and over the tied pairs, stick pin in front, return with "Cloth" stitch, twist worker twice, pin at the top of the petal, "Cloth" stitch behind pin, twist both pairs twice, leave outer pair and "Cloth" stitch through with inner pair. Pass the worker under and over tied pairs, pin, return with "Cloth" stitch, twist worker twice, pin at the top of petal, "Cloth" stitch behind pin, twist both pairs twice, leave outer pair and "Cloth" stitch through with inner pair, pass the worker under and over tied pairs, pin, return with "Cloth" stitch, twist worker twice, pin at the top of petal, "Cloth" stitch behind pin, twist both pairs twice, leave outer pair and "Cloth" stitch through with inner pair, pass the worker under and over tied pairs, pin ; return with "Cloth" stitch, twist worker twice, pin at the top of petal; "Cloth" stitch behind pin, twist both pairs twice, leave outer pair and "Cloth" stitch through with inner pair, pass the worker under and over tied pairs, pin, return with "Cloth" stitch, twist worker twice, pin at the top of the petal; "Cloth" stitch behind pin, twist both pairs twice, leave outer pair and "Cloth" stitch through with inner pair, pass the worker under and over tied pairs, pin, return with "Cloth" stitch, twist worker twice, pin at division of petal; "Cloth" stitch behind pin, twist both pairs twice, leave; twist each pair of passives once to the left;* repeat from * to *. Work "Cloth" stitch and an extra twist with the inner pair down to the ring, pass the working pair under and over the tied bobbins, stick pin in front and leave; start with the 2nd pair of bobbins from the top, "Cloth" stitch with 3rd pair, twist right-hand pair once, left-hand pair twice, stick pin at the top of the petal, "Cloth" stitch, twist both pairs twice; start with the 2nd pair and work "Cloth" stitch and an extra twist down to the ring passing the working pair under and over the tied pairs, stick a pin in front and leave. Commence with the 2nd and 3rd pair at the top of the petal, "Cloth" stitch, twist right-hand pair once and the left-hand pair twice, stick pin at the top of the petal, "Cloth" stitch behind pin, twisting both pairs twice, work "Cloth" stitch and an extra twist with the 2nd pair down to the ring and leave, repeat this a second time through 5 pairs, repeat a third time through 4 pairs, repeat again through 3 pairs and again through 2 pairs. "Cloth" stitch with the 2nd and 3rd pair at the top of the petal, twist the right-hand pair once and the left-hand pair twice, stick pin at the top of the petal and work "Cloth" stitch at the back of the pin, twisting both pairs twice, leave; stick pin between 3rd and 4th pairs, "Cloth" stitch round pin, leave, repeat with 5th and 6th pairs, repeat with 7th and 8th pairs, leave; "Cloth" stitch with 2nd pair through 3rd and 4th pairs, twist the worker once and work "Cloth" stitch through 5th and 6th pairs, twist the workers once and work "Cloth" stitch through 7th and 8th pairs, twist the workers once and pass under and over tied pairs, pin in front. This finishes the flower, being the fifth petal, so take all the pins out of the ring of flower and tie the 4 tied bobbins to the end of the thread left when starting.

Continue to work the stem by passing the 4 tied bobbins over and under each pair of bobbins, leave; "Cloth" stitch with 7th and 8th pairs, connect 8th pair into the 1st petal, tie; "Cloth" stitch through 7th and 6th pairs, leave 6th pair; "Cloth" stitch with 7th and 8th pairs, connect with 8th pair,

tie ; " Cloth " stitch with 7th and 8th pairs ; " Cloth " stitch
with 6th and 7th pairs ; " Cloth " stitch with 6th and 5th
pairs, leave 5th pair ; " Cloth " stitch with 6th and 7th,
also 7th and 8th pairs, connect 8th pair, tie ; " Cloth "
stitch with 7th and 8th pairs, 6th and 7th pairs, 5th and 6th
pairs, 4th and 5th pairs, leave 4th pair ; " Cloth " stitch
with 5th and 6th pairs, 6th and 7th pairs, 7th and 8th pairs,
connect 8th pair, tie ; " Cloth " stitch with 7th and 8th
pairs, 6th and 7th pairs, 5th and 6th pairs, 4th and 5th
pairs, 3rd and 4th pairs, leave 3rd pair ; " Cloth " stitch
with 4th and 5th pairs, 5th and 6th pairs, 6th and 7th pairs,
7th and 8th pairs, connect 8th pair into the top of 1st petal,
tie ; " Cloth " stitch with 7th and 8th pairs, twist both pairs
twice, pin in front, leave outer pair and " Cloth " stitch
with inner pair through all the pairs, pass the working pair
under the tied pairs, connect, tie ; pass the working pair
over the tied pairs, pin ; " Cloth " stitch through all the
passives, twist the working pair twice, pin ; " Cloth " stitch
behind pin, twist both pairs twice, leave outer pair ;
" Cloth " stitch through with the 2nd pair, pass the working
pair under and over the tied pairs, pin ; " Cloth " stitch
through all the passives, twist the working pair twice, pin ;
" Cloth " stitch behind pin, twist both pairs twice, leave
outer pair ; " Cloth " stitch with 2nd pair, continue working

the stem until you arrive at the first strand, which is worked as follows : pass the working pair under the tied pairs, twisting it until it reaches the petal, connect, tie and twist until you reach half-way up the strand, connect in the strand, tie, twist it three times to form the picot, stick a pin under the thread of the outer bobbin, twist once and pin down, now twist the thread of the inner bobbin once round the pin and twist the pair three times, connect to the strand, tie, and twist until they reach the tied pairs, passing this pair over the tied pairs, pin and continue to work the stem until you reach the next strand.

The small leaves are worked in the " Venetian " stitch, the stems and scrolls in " Cloth " stitch.

The little fancy edging bordering the Collar is worked with 6 pairs of bobbins.

Stick a pin in each of the three lines indicated on the working Pattern, hang 1 pair of bobbins on the 1st pin, left hand, 1 pair on the 2nd pin, 4 pairs on the 3rd pin ; commence working " Cloth " stitch with the 1st and 2nd pairs, leave 1st pair, " Cloth " stitch through with the 2nd pair ; " Plait " stitch with the 5th and 6th pairs, making the picots on each dot ; work " Plait " stitch until you arrive at the traced square, work " Cloth " stitch with the 3rd and 4th pairs, twist both pairs twice, twist 2nd pair

twice; "Cloth" stitch with the 2nd and 3rd pairs, twist
both pairs twice, twist the 1st pair twice; "Cloth" stitch
with the 1st and 2nd pairs, twist both pairs twice, pin in
front of 2nd pair; "Cloth" stitch with 2nd and 3rd pairs,
twist both pairs twice; "Cloth" stitch with 3rd and 4th
pairs, twist 3rd pair twice and the 4th pair three times,
picot; "Cloth" stitch with 3rd and 4th pairs, twist both
pairs twice; "Cloth" stitch with 2nd and 3rd pairs, twist
both pairs twice; "Cloth" stitch with 1st and 2nd pairs,
twist both pairs twice, pin in front of 2nd pair; "Cloth"
stitch with 2nd and 3rd pairs; "Cloth" stitch with 3rd
and 4th pairs; "Cloth" stitch with 4th and 5th pairs;
"Cloth" stitch with 5th and 6th pairs, pin on square;
"Cloth" stitch with 5th and 6th pairs round pin; "Cloth"
stitch with 4th and 5th pairs; "Cloth" stitch with 3rd and
4th pairs; "Cloth" stitch with 2nd and 3rd pairs, twist
2nd pair twice; "Cloth" stitch with 1st and 2nd pairs,
twist both pairs twice, pin in front of 2nd pair; "Cloth"
stitch through with 2nd pair, twist worker once, pin on
square; "Cloth" stitch round pin, leave outer pair and
work "Cloth" stitch through with inner pair until you
arrive at the twisted pair, twist worker twice; "Cloth"
stitch with 1st and 2nd pairs, twist both pairs twice, pin in
front of 2nd pair; "Cloth" stitch through with 2nd pair,

pin on square ; " Cloth " stitch round pin, *twist 4th and 5th pairs twice ; " Cloth " stitch with 4th and 5th pairs, twist 4th pair twice, twist 3rd pair twice ; " Cloth " stitch with 3rd and 4th pairs, twist both pairs twice, twist 2nd pair twice ; " Cloth " stitch with 2nd and 3rd pairs, twist both pairs twice ; " Cloth " stitch with 1st and 2nd pairs, twist both pairs twice, pin in front of 2nd pair ; " Cloth " stitch with 2nd and 3rd pairs, twist both pairs twice ; " Cloth " stitch with 3rd and 4th pairs, twist 3rd pair twice and 4th pair three times, picot ; " Cloth " stitch with 3rd and 4th pairs, twist both pairs twice ; " Cloth " stitch with 2nd and 3rd pairs, twist both pairs twice ; " Cloth " stitch with 1st and 2nd pairs, twist both pairs twice, pin in front of 2nd pair ; " Cloth " stitch with 2nd and 3rd pairs ; " Cloth " stitch with 3rd and 4th pairs, leave ; " Plait " stitch with 5th and 6th pairs, making picots on each dot, until you arrive at traced square ; " Cloth " stitch with 4th and 5th pairs ; " Cloth " stitch with 5th and 6th pairs, pin between 5th and 6th pairs on square ; " Cloth " stitch round pin ; " Cloth " stitch with 4th and 5th pairs ; " Cloth " stitch with 3rd and 4th pairs ; " Cloth " stitch with 2nd and 3rd pairs, twist 2nd pair twice ; " Cloth " stitch with 1st and 2nd pairs, twist both pairs twice, pin in front of 2nd pair ; " Cloth " stitch through with 2nd pair, twist worker once, pin on square; " Cloth" stitch round pin, leave outer pair and "Cloth" stitch through with inner pair until you arrive at twisted pair, twist worker twice; "Cloth" stitch with 1st and 2nd pairs, twist both pairs twice, pin in front of 2nd pair; "Cloth" stitch through with 2nd pair, pin on square; "Cloth" stitch round pin,* repeat from * to *.

N.B.—These directions are given for commencing at the left-hand point of Collar, as indicated in the working Pattern.

## FLOUNCE IN OLD FLEMISH LACE

The Old Flemish Flounce illustrated under the Venetian lace is $4\frac{1}{2}$ inches wide, it is worked in size 3 thread without cord. This is a very interesting Pattern, the braid outline of the Flowers and Leaves being interspersed with Windows, Open Veins and Double Reseau. Directions for working the two latter are given on pages 57 and 156; the Windows (a series of tiny square openings) are made by twisting the two middle passive bobbins twice, and also twisting the working pair twice before and after working through these, for the 2nd row twist the working pair only, and for the 3rd row the two passive bobbins.

The Hexagon net background is worked last with separate bobbins connecting two pairs of bobbins at each division of the net (indicated on the working Pattern), plait down to the end of the little line, stick a pin here, work " Cloth " stitch and repeat to the end of the row or section, now take one pair from each plait, twist several times until they reach the next row of lines, work " Cloth " stitch, stick a pin on the top of the line. Plait to the bottom, stick a pin, " Cloth ' stitch, and so on until the whole of the space is worked.

## MILANESE D'OYLEY

The Milanese D'Oyley measures 6 inches across and is
worked in size 2 thread, it can be used for a variety of
purposes, and also forms a very handsome crown for a hat.
The working directions are as follows :—

Commence in the centre of the D'Oyley with eleven pairs
of bobbins, working ordinary " Cloth " stitch braid with the
open edge until you arrive at the dot indicated in the traced
Pattern.  Twist the working pair three times (you will have
five pairs of bobbins on either side of the working pair).
On your return, twist the 5th pair of bobbins three times ;
make a " Cloth " stitch ; twist the working pair three times,
and twist your stitch pair three times.  The bars in the
centre are done in " Plait " stitch with a picot at each point.
When you arrive at the line traced on the braid, twist every
pair of bobbins three times, except the working pair.  The
fancy inlet of *double reseau* in this braid is worked as
follows :—After you have made your twice-twist, and put
in the pin at the right-hand side of the top small line, work

D'Oyley and Collar in Milanese Lace ; also Flounce in Old Milanese.

For full size pattern of D'Oyley see folding sheet 1.

"Cloth" stitch behind pin, twist both pairs twice, leave the two twisted pairs, and twist a 3rd pair of bobbins once. Now take the 4th and 5th pairs of bobbins, work " Cloth " stitch, and put pin in 1st dot (indicated in the prepared Pattern). Work " Cloth " stitch. Drop these, and take up the 6th and 7th pairs, " Cloth " stitch, pin in 2nd dot, " Cloth " stitch, drop these, and take up the 8th and 9th pairs, " Cloth " stitch, pin in 3rd dot, " Cloth " stitch, drop these, take the 10th pair, twist once, drop these, and *take the 2nd and 3rd pairs on your right-hand side and make a " Cloth " stitch, drop the 2nd pair, twist the 3rd pair twice, work a " Cloth " stitch through the 4th and 5th pairs, twist your workers twice, make a " Cloth " stitch through the next two pairs, repeat once more, twist your workers twice, make a " Cloth " stitch with the next pair, twist the workers twice, stick a pin in between the two small lines in front of the workers, *i.e.*, your two pairs of bobbins behind the pin, make "Cloth " stitch, twist both pairs twice, leave the out-side twisted pair, return with your 2nd pair, making a " Cloth " stitch with the 2nd and 3rd pairs, twist the workers twice and work back to your right-hand side in the same manner as the previous row ; now put your pin in the lowest small line, "Cloth" stitch behind pin, twist both pairs twice, leave these, take up the 3rd pair, twist once and drop

K

these, take up the 4th and 5th pairs, " Cloth " stitch, pin in
1st dot, " Cloth " stitch, drop these, take 6th and 7th pairs,
" Cloth " stitch, pin in 2nd dot, " Cloth " stitch, take up the
8th and 9th pairs, " Cloth " stitch, pin in the 3rd dot,
" Cloth " stitch, drop these, twist the 10th pair once, drop
these, go back to the right-hand side, take up the 2nd and
3rd pair, make a " Cloth " stitch, twist both pairs twice,
drop the 2nd pair, twist the 4th pair twice, make " Cloth "
stitch with 3rd and 4th pairs, stick pin in 1st dot, " Cloth "
stitch, twist both pairs twice, drop these, take up the next
two pairs, twist twice, " Cloth " stitch, pin in 2nd dot, " Cloth "
stitch, twist both pairs twice, drop these, take up the next
two pairs, twist twice, " Cloth " stitch, pin in 3rd dot, " Cloth "
stitch, twist both pairs twice, drop these, take up the next
pair, twist twice and work " Cloth " stitch with it and the
last pair but one, twist both pairs twice, drop these and work
" Cloth " stitch with the two other pairs, stick pin in front of
stitch on 4th dot, twist both pairs twice, leave the outer
twisted pair, make " Cloth " stitch with the 2nd and 3rd
pairs, twist both pairs twice, drop these ; now take the 3rd
pair of bobbins on the right-hand side, work " Cloth " stitch
with these and the 2nd pair, twist both pairs twice, drop the
3rd pair, work " Cloth " stitch with the 1st and 2nd pairs,
twist both pairs twice, stick pin in front of stitch (on the top

small line), drop these, take the 4th and 5th pairs, " Cloth " stitch, pin in 1st dot, " Cloth " stitch, drop these, take up 6th and 7th pairs, " Cloth " stitch, pin in 2nd dot, " Cloth " stitch, drop these, take up the 8th and 9th pairs, " Cloth " stitch, pin in the 3rd dot, " Cloth " stitch, drop these, go back to the right-hand side and repeat from *.

The Reseau and Old Flanders Fillings are used in this D'Oyley, the working details of these stitches being given on pages 52 and 143.

## MILANESE LACE COLLAR

The Milanese Pomegranate Collar is 5 inches deep and worked in size 4 thread; no cord is used in this lace.

The outline of the design is worked first, using on an average eight pairs of bobbins. This outline, which is worked like the braid in Point de Flandres, is carried round all the flowers, leaves and scrolls, which are afterwards filled in with a variety of fancy stitches—" Reseau," " Double Reseau," " Fine Honeycomb" and " Half" stitch—as indicated on the working Pattern; all these stitches have already been described on pages 52, 57, and 150.

## FLOUNCE IN OLD MILANESE

This Flounce is a copy of a very old design in the possession of one of our pupils, who reproduced this lace under our tuition. The original flounce, which is 6 inches deep, had been used on a wedding-dress. It is worked in size 3 thread, without cord; the braid is worked first, and requires on an average nine pairs of bobbins.

This lace can also be used for church decoration, and makes a beautiful Altar Frontal; in this case it is advisable to work it in rather coarser thread—size 2.

The net background in this lace is worked as described in the Old Flemish Flounce, page 125.

## VANDYKE COLLAR IN FLEMISH LACE

The Flemish Vandyke Collar ($5\frac{1}{2}$ inches deep) is worked in size 2 thread, but the finer Bruges cord is substituted in place of the heavier Guipure cord, a single outline of this finer cord being carried round the outside of the braid and scrolls as well as the flowers and leaves. The little round fancy holes that occur so frequently in the "Cloth" stitch portions of the design are made as follows: on arriving at the place where the hole is indicated on the working Pattern, twist the working pair of bobbins three times in the middle of the row, and on the return row twist the nearest passive pair three times before working through it, twist the working pair three times, also the next passive pair.

These fancy holes are very much used for ornamenting all kinds of lace, and occur very often in flowers and leaves as well as in the scrolls and fancy shapes. The "Reseau" filling is used in the lower part of the Vandykes,

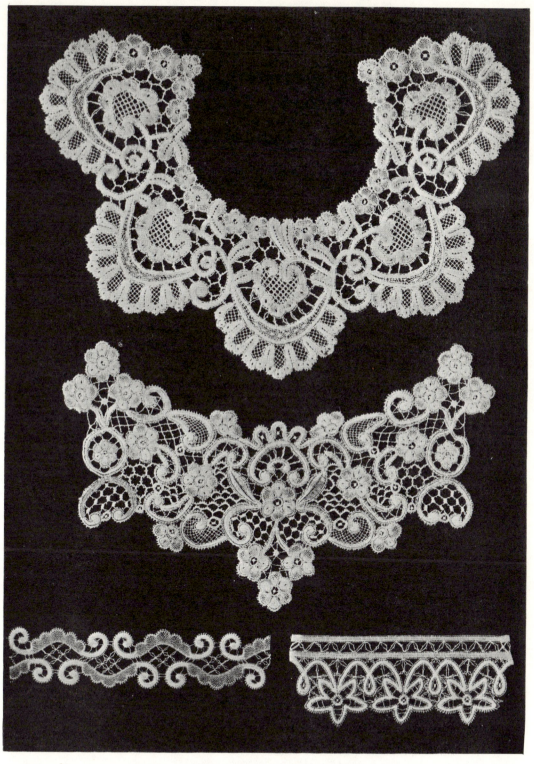

Vandyke Collar in Flemish Lace ; Yoke Piece in Guipure de Flandre ; Insertion in Point de Flandre ; Lace Edge in Italian (Genoese).

whilst in the upper part an elaborate stitch known as the "Spot" insertion is introduced. To work this, connect one pair of bobbins each side of the braid, twist three times "Cloth" stitch, pin in middle of stitch at top of first lozenge indicated in working Pattern, twist both pairs three times; leave these, connect two more pairs a little lower down, twist three times, and work "Cloth" stitch with these and the first two pairs at each side of the lozenge, with pin in middle of each "Cloth" stitch, twist all four pairs three times; hang two pairs on a little lower down, twist three times, work "Cloth" stitch with nearest pair each side of lozenge, with pin in middle of each stitch, twist all these three times; "Cloth" stitch with two centre pairs, "Cloth" stitch with 3rd and 4th pairs both sides, "Cloth" stitch with two centre pairs, connect two more pairs of bobbins, twist three times, work "Cloth" stitch, with pin in middle, with the two outside pairs, and twist all four pairs three times; work "Cloth" stitch with the 2nd and 3rd pair, each side, and the 3rd and 4th, "Cloth" stitch the two middle pairs; now work "Cloth" stitch backwards with the 4th and 3rd pairs, repeat with the 3rd and 2nd, twist the 2nd pair three times; work "Cloth" stitch, pin in middle, with the outside twisted pair, and twist both pairs three times.

Work the other side in the same manner; return to the centre, work "Cloth" stitch with the two centre pairs, "Cloth" stitch with 4th and 3rd pairs, twist the latter pair three times; work "Cloth" stitch with this and 2nd pair with pin in middle of stitch on 6th dot, twist both pairs three times. Work the other side in the same manner; return to middle and make "Cloth" stitch with the two centre pairs, twist both pairs three times; now work "Cloth" stitch with 3rd and 4th pairs, pin in middle of stitch on 7th dot, twist three times. Again repeat on other side; "Cloth" stitch with two middle pairs, pin in middle of stitch on bottom of lozenge, twist both pairs three times; for the second spot connect the first twisted pair into the braid, twist three times, and work "Cloth" stitch with next twisted pair, twist both pairs three times, drop the first pair, work through the next pair, twist both three times. Repeat on the opposite side; return to 3rd and 4th pairs, work "Cloth" stitch with pin in middle of stitch, twist both pairs three times. Repeat on other side; connect the first twisted pair into the braid, twist three times, and work "Cloth" stitch with next twisted pair, twist both pairs three times; "Cloth" stitch with 2nd and 3rd pairs, pin in middle of stitch, twist both pairs three times. Repeat on other side; connect 1st pair into braid and twist three times; "Cloth" stitch with pin in middle of stitch, twist both pairs three times. Repeat on other side; work from * to *.

For the third spot connect the first twisted pair into the braid, twist three times, work "Cloth" stitch with 1st and 2nd pairs, twist both pairs three times, leave 1st pair; repeat with next pair, twist both pairs three times; repeat on the opposite side, "Cloth" stitch with 3rd and 4th pairs, stick pin in middle of stitch, twist both pairs three times; repeat on opposite side, connect the first twisted pair into the braid, twist three times, work "Cloth" stitch with the next twisted pair, twist both pairs three times, work "Cloth" stitch with 2nd and 3rd pairs, stick pin in middle of stitch, twist both pairs three times; repeat on other side, connect 1st pair into the braid, twist three times, work "Cloth" stitch with 2nd pair, stick pin in the middle of stitch, twist both pairs three times; repeat on the other side, * work "Cloth" stitch with the two centre pairs, work "Cloth" stitch with 3rd and 4th pairs both sides, "Cloth" stitch with two centre pairs, work "Cloth" stitch with 2nd and 3rd pairs both sides, also with the 3rd and 4th pairs, work "Cloth" stitch with the two middle pairs; now work "Cloth" stitch with the 4th and 3rd pairs; repeat with the 3rd and 2nd pairs, twist the 2nd pair three times; work "Cloth" stitch, pin in middle with outside twisted pair, and twist both pairs three times. Work the other side in the same manner; return to the centre; work "Cloth" stitch with the two centre pairs, "Cloth" stitch with 4th and 3rd pairs, twist the latter pair three times; work "Cloth" stitch with this and 2nd pair, stick pin in middle of stitch on 6th dot, twist both pairs three times. Work the other side in the same manner; return to the middle and work "Cloth" stitch with the two centre pairs, twist both pairs three times; now work "Cloth" stitch with 3rd and 4th pairs, pin in middle of stitch on 7th dot, twist both pairs three times. Again repeat on the other side; work "Cloth" stitch with two middle pairs, pin in middle of stitch on bottom of lozenge, twist both pairs three times.*

For the fourth spot connect the first twisted pair into the braid, twist three times, work "Cloth" stitch with 1st and 2nd pairs, twist both pairs three times, leave 1st pair; repeat with next pair, twist both pairs three times; repeat on the opposite side, work "Cloth" stitch with 3rd and 4th pairs, stick pin in middle of stitch, twist both pairs three times; repeat on opposite side, connect the first twisted pair into the braid, twist three times, work "Cloth" stitch with the next twisted pair, twist both pairs three times, work " Cloth " stitch with 2nd and 3rd pairs, stick pin in middle of stitch, twist both pairs three times ; repeat on other side, connect 1st pair into the braid, twist three times, work " Cloth " stitch with 2nd pair, stick pin in the middle of stitch, twist both pairs three times ; repeat on the other side, repeat from * to *.

For the fifth spot connect the first twisted pair into the braid, twist three times, work " Cloth " stitch with 1st and 2nd pairs, twist both pairs three times, leave 1st pair ; repeat with next pair, twist both pairs three times ; repeat on the opposite side, work " Cloth " stitch with 3rd and 4th pairs, stick pin in middle of stitch, twist both pairs three times ; repeat on opposite side, connect the first twisted pair into the braid, twist three times, work " Cloth " stitch with the next twisted pair, twist both pairs three times, work " Cloth " stitch with 2nd and 3rd pairs, stick pin in the middle of stitch, twist both pairs three times ; repeat on other side, connect first pair into the braid, twist three times, work " Cloth " stitch with 2nd pair, stick pin in the middle of stitch, twist both pairs three times ; repeat on the other side, repeat from * to *.

For the sixth spot connect the first twisted pair into the braid, twist three times, work " Cloth " stitch with 1st and 2nd pairs, twist both pairs three times, leave 1st pair; repeat with next pair, twist both pairs three times; repeat on the opposite side, work " Cloth " stitch with 3rd and 4th pairs, stick pin in middle of stitch, twist both pairs three times; repeat on opposite side, connect the first twisted pair into the braid, twist three times, work " Cloth " stitch with the next twisted pair, twist both pairs three times, work " Cloth " stitch with 2nd and 3rd pairs, stick pin in the middle of stitch, twist both pairs three times; repeat on other side, connect 1st pair into the braid, twist three times, work " Cloth " stitch with 2nd pair, stick pin in the middle of stitch, twist both pairs three times; repeat on the other side, repeat from * to *.

For the seventh spot connect the first twisted pair into the braid, twist three times, work " Cloth " stitch with 1st and 2nd pairs, twist both pairs three times, leave 1st pair; repeat with next pair, twist both pairs three times; repeat on opposite side, work " Cloth " stitch with 3rd and 4th pairs, stick pin in middle of stitch, twist both pairs three times; repeat on opposite side, connect the first twisted pair into the braid, twist three times, work " Cloth " stitch with the next twisted pair, twist both pairs three times, work " Cloth " stitch with 2nd and 3rd pairs, stick pin in middle of stitch, twist both pairs three times; repeat on other side, connect 1st pair into the braid, twist three times, work "Cloth" stitch with 2nd pair, stick pin in the middle of stitch, twist both pairs three times: repeat on the other side.

For the large medallions in this Collar the "Old Flandres" filling is used; this is quickly worked; connect two pairs of bobbins at the top of each square (one pair each side of the lines) indicated on the working Pattern, twist each pair once, work "Half" stitch, stick pin in between (on line near the cross), now connect two extra pairs at this cross-line and work with these through the entire row, in the following manner: twist both these pairs once, work "Half" stitch, stick pin in between the stitch on this line (near the cross), work "Cloth" stitch with the 2nd and 3rd pairs (reckoning from the right hand) and twist both pairs once; "Cloth" stitch with 1st and 2nd pairs, twist both pairs once; "Cloth" stitch with 3rd and 4th pairs, twist both pairs once, stick pin on the left line of cross between the 3rd and 4th pairs, "Cloth" stitch with 2nd and 3rd pairs, twist both pairs once, stick pin on the lower cross-line, between 1st and 2nd pairs, work "Half" stitch with 1st and 2nd pairs, stick pin in between stitch on same line at the next cross, work "Half" stitch with 3rd and 4th pairs, pin in between stitch on line at cross underneath.

## YOKE IN GUIPURE DE FLANDRE

The directions given for Guipure de Flandre on pages 41 to 48 are to be followed for working this Yoke. The " Reseau," " Honeycomb," " Spider Web," and " Festoon " fillings, illustrated with full working directions on pages 53 to 61, are all employed in this yoke, which is 7 inches deep and forms a very beautiful trimming across the front of a blouse or bodice. The cuffs and collar-band can be worked to match if desired. We have also a very handsome panel for the front of the skirt in this design ; this panel is 21 inches deep, 15 inches wide at the foot, tapering upwards to a point.

This lace is worked in size 2 thread, outlined with Guipure cord. A single cord is used for outlining the flowers, and a pair of cords for all the scrolls. The large leaves in the middle of the design are worked as described on pages 152 to 156.

## INSERTION IN POINT DE FLANDRE

The directions given for the Point de Flandre lace
(pages 19 to 38) can be followed for this Insertion, which
is 2 inches wide and suitable for a great many purposes.
Worked in rather coarse thread (size 1), it makes a very
handsome trimming for cushion covers, table centres, &c.,
and for this purpose we have a corner design to match.
If worked in No. 2 or 3 thread, it forms a very beautiful
trimming for frocks and blouses.

The whole design has a cord outline, a pair of cord
bobbins being used for this purpose. The plaited fillings
are worked as arrived at and connected together where
the lines cross each other on the working Pattern.

## ITALIAN LACE EDGE (GENOESE)

This Italian Lace Edge (3½ inches wide) is worked exactly like the first pattern in the book (page 13) and without cord.  Any length of this lace can be worked in one piece without leaving off.  It is the easiest of all laces to make, and although this is a very simple pattern, it makes a very effective trimming for Afternoon Tea Cloths, Table Centres, Altar Cloths, &c.

The Strands or connecting bars in the lace are thrown out whilst proceeding, those in the flowers being twisted, and the others plaited.

Cravat with Collar Band in Flemish Lace ; Revers Collar in Old Flemish ; also *Appliqué*
Lace Trimming.

## FLEMISH LACE FRONT WITH COLLAR-BAND

In the Flemish lace the heavy Guipure cord is omitted and the finer Bruges cord substituted in its place. This cord is worked as described in Point de Flandre, but the rest of the work is similar to Guipure de Flandre. The stitches already given—" Reseau," " Spider Web," " Festoon," and " Honeycomb " (pages 52 and 57)—are employed in this Lace Front and Collar, which is worked in size 3 thread.

## REVERS COLLAR IN OLD FLEMISH

The principal " Fillings " in this Collar (which is 5 inches wide) are the " Double Reseau," " Large Net," and " Fine Honeycomb," the two former stitches have already been described on pages 60 and 162. The " Fine Honeycomb " is worked in the six leaves bordering the Collar and is done as follows: Connect two pairs of bobbins into the braid at the top of each dot (indicated on the working Pattern), work " Half " stitch and an extra twist, pin in dot, " Half " stitch and an extra twist; *connect a fresh pair of bobbins into the right-hand side of the braid at the next row of dots, twist twice, " Half " stitch and an extra twist, pin, " Half " stitch and an extra twist, repeat to the end of the row ; connect a fresh pair of bobbins at the right-hand side of the braid, twist twice, " Half " stitch and an extra twist, pin, " Half " stitch and an extra twist, drop these bobbins and repeat with the next two pairs, and so on to the end of the row.* For the following row repeat the directions from * to *. This Collar is worked in size 2 thread outlined with Bruges cord to correspond.

## FLEMISH LACE TRIMMING

This *Appliqué* Lace Trimming is $3\frac{1}{2}$ inches deep and can be used for a variety of purposes.

It is worked in size 2 thread outlined with Bruges cord to correspond.

The "Honeycomb," "Piqué," and "Plaited Fillings" are employed in this lace; directions for these stitches have been given on pages 53 and 157.

The edge of this lace is worked quite differently to the ordinary picots, it is known as the "Loop" edge, and is made by simply bringing the outer pair of bobbins (which are twisted three times as for ordinary picots) round the pin, "Cloth" stitch, twist both pairs twice before passing the cord, and proceed as usual.

## FLOUNCE AND BERTHÈ IN DUCHESSE LACE

The Duchesse Berthè (5½ inches deep), of which one half is shown on the illustration, and the Duchesse Flounce (6 inches deep) are both worked in size 3 thread with Bruges cord to correspond. The large flowers in the Berthè as well as the centre scroll in the Flounce have a filling of "Half" stitch, which is put in separately like the other fillings. Some of the leaves in both the Flounce and Berthè are worked like the Flandres leaves described on pages 24 and 25, and some are worked straight across in one piece. For these latter commence with seven pairs of bobbins, stick two pins at the top of the leaf, hang three pairs on the right-hand pin one by one and work "Cloth" stitch with each, twist the two outer pairs twice, take the outside pair round the back of the other pin, hang the remaining four pairs on this pin and work "Cloth" stitch through these with the second pair of the first three pairs, have ready a pair of bobbins wound with cord and pin

Duchesse Lace Berthè and Flounce; also Table Centre in Flemish Lace.

this down a little way from the top of the leaf, pass the left-hand cord bobbin through the working pair and the right-hand cord through the next four pairs of bobbins; now return to the working pair at the left hand, twist twice, stick pin in front in the same hole as the commencing pin, " Cloth " stitch with this and the outside pair, twist both pairs twice, pass the cord through the inner pair, work " Cloth " stitch right across to opposite cord, pass this through the working pair, twist twice, stick pin in the same hole as the commencing pin at this side; " Cloth " stitch, twist both pairs twice, pass the cord; " Cloth " stitch across to the opposite cord, pass this, now take out the three commencing pins, pull all the threads and cords gently into position so that no loops are left, carefully move the left-hand pin to the extreme tip point of the leaf, twist the working pair twice, stick pin in the same hole as the previous pin which you have just removed; " Cloth " stitch, twist twice, pin the cord firmly down at the tip of leaf to prevent this slipping, pass the cord through the working pair; " Cloth " stitch across to the opposite cord, pass the cord, twist twice, pin in front; " Cloth" stitch, twist both pairs twice, pass the cord through the inner pair; " Cloth " stitch across to the opposite cord, pass this, twist twice, pin opposite last pin and repeat until you arrive at the vein, adding two pairs of bobbins on each of the next two rows to make eleven pairs ; to add extra bobbins hang a new pair on a pin placed close to the cord on the inside, and work as usual. For the open vein "Cloth" stitch through four pairs of bobbins, twist the working pair three times, "Cloth" stitch through the remaining four pairs and repeat this every row to the end of the vein.

## TABLE CENTRE IN FLEMISH LACE

The Flemish Table Centre, of which one quarter is illustrated, is worked in No. 2 thread, outlined with Bruges cord to match. It is mounted on rich white silk and is 24 inches square when finished ; the depth of the lace corner is 9 inches. We also have this design in an Afternoon Tea Cloth, 36 inches square. The directions given for Point de Flandre can be followed for this design, except for the flowers with the open vein in the middle of the petals, which is made by twisting all the pairs of passive bobbins twice, work " Cloth " stitch with these and twist twice again. It will be noticed that the cord is not carried down the sides of the petals in these flowers. The fillings in this table centre are very hand-some ; they include the " Diamond," " Reseau," and " Piqué," the two former are described on pages 53 and 59.

The Piqué Filling is worked in exactly the same

manner as the Woven Bar Filling described on page 162, except that the threads are plaited (with a picot each side) instead of woven, and the two pairs of bobbins are connected *close together* at the top of each line (indicated on the working Pattern), instead of *apart*, as in the Woven Bar Filling.

Puritan Collar, Neck Band, Motifs, Fan and Lace Edge in Honiton Lace.

For full size patterns of Neck Band, Fan and Lace Edge (with corner)
see folding sheet 2.

## HONITON FAN

The exquisite Honiton Fan, illustrated on page 160, measures 14½ inches across from end to end, and is 4½ inches deep. It is worked in size 4 thread with gimp to correspond. A great deal of the "raised" work is employed in the working of this fan. Start with five pairs of bobbins and work all the veins of the leaves in the "raised" cord as described on pages 77 to 81, the same "raised" cord is continued all round the extreme edge of the leaves, which are then filled in with "Half" stitch and "Cloth" stitch in alternate sections; the "Half" stitch sections require eleven pairs of bobbins and the "Cloth" stitch nine pairs. Each section is worked right across in one piece, connecting each row to the veins as well as to the raised cord at the edges of the leaf. The flowers bordering the fan are also done in raised work, whilst the clusters of flowers in the middle and at each side of the fan are worked with the open vein (as described in the Flemish Table Centre). Ten pairs of bobbins and one single gimp bobbin are used for these flowers. The stems have the raised cord on one side and gimp on the other side ; five pairs of bobbins and one gimp bobbin are sufficient for these stems. The "Woven Bar" filling in the centre medallion of the fan is worked as follows : Connect 1 pair of bobbins on each side of the lines indicated in the working Pattern at the top, twist each pair twice and weave a bar (as described in the lead filling, page 56) with the two pairs nearest the right hand, stick a pin between (on the line) and twist both pairs twice ; work another bar in the same manner on the nearest cross line, stick a pin between and twist both pairs twice, work a "Cloth" stitch with the two middle pairs, twist each pair twice, work "Cloth" stitch with the two right-hand pairs and twist each pair twice ; repeat with the two left-hand pairs, stick a pin between these on the cross line, work a "Cloth" stitch with the two middle pairs, twist each pair twice and now stick a pin between the two right-hand pairs on the line under the first pin just below the cross.

The fan has a bobbin net ground known as the Large and Small Mesh ; to work the former connect two pairs of bobbins at the right-hand side of the second row of dots indicating the net and work four "Plait" stitches ; connect two pairs of bobbins at the nearest dot on the first row of the net, *work four " Plait " stitches, work " Cloth " stitch with the two middle pairs of the four pairs ; repeat with the two left-hand pairs and stick pin between the two middle pairs (the pin to be on the nearest dot in the second row), work four " Plait " stitches with each two pairs, connect on two more pairs* and repeat from * to * with the two pairs of bobbins at the left hand, whilst the two right-hand pairs will be worked in the next row and are left ready plaited.

For the Small Mesh net connect one pair of bobbins at the right-hand side of the second row of dots indicated on the working Pattern, and twist this pair three times ; now connect a pair of bobbins at the nearest dot in the top row of net, twist this pair three times, work " Half" stitch with this and the other twisted pair, pin in between stitch on the nearest dot in the second row, twist both pairs twice, connect another pair of bobbins on next dot in top row of net, twist three times, work " Half" stitch with this and the nearest pair of bobbins, pin in the next dot of the second row of net, twist each pair twice, and so on to the end of the row, the return row being worked in the same manner.

## HONITON COLLARS

The Honiton Neck Band (Hawthorn design) is $2\frac{1}{4}$ inches deep, and the little Puritan Collar $1\frac{1}{2}$ inches deep; there is no raised work in these collars, which are worked in size 4 thread and gimp to correspond. The centre medallion in the Hawthorn collar has an open vein that is worked in the same way as the leaf described on page 24 ; the blossoms are worked in " Cloth " stitch, with six pairs of bobbins and one gimp ; the leaves are worked one side " Half " stitch and the other side " Cloth " stitch, with the exception of the very small leaves, which are worked entirely in " Cloth " stitch.

The " Reseau " filling, described on page 53, is used in the little Puritan collar, and the fancy braid at the top of the collar is worked as described on page 69.

## HONITON *MOTIFS*

The two Honiton *Motifs*, if worked in size 4 thread, are useful for ornamenting elegant Blouses and Frocks, or, worked a little coarser, they can be used for appliquéing on linen Frocks, Cushion Covers, &c.

The oval *Motif* measures 3 inches by $2\frac{1}{4}$ inches, and the round *Motif* is $2\frac{1}{2}$ inches across. Raised cord is made on one side of the leaves in the oval *Motif*, which is worked entirely in " Cloth " stitch with a background of " Plait " stitch. There is no raised work in the round *Motif ;* the fancy braid round the border is worked in " Half " stitch, and this is connected to the flower with " Spider Webs ; " the flower is filled in with " Reseau," and " Lead filling " in the centre. The working of all these stitches is described on pages 17, 18, 53 and 57.

## HONITON LACE EDGE

This Honiton Lace Edge is 3½ inches wide, and is worked in size 4 thread with gimp to correspond. The "roses" and "jessamine" are worked as described on pages 64 and 67, in "Cloth" stitch; the jessamine leaves are also worked in "Cloth" stitch, but with the "raised" cord; both varieties of raised cord are used in these leaves, viz., "worked" and "tied," the former, which has already been described on page 77, is worked right up the middle of the leaf, whilst for each little division the tied cord is used. Full directions for working these leaves are given on page 100. The larger leaves are worked one side "Cloth" stitch and one side "Half" stitch.

The braid at the top of the lace is made with the Honiton Bars, as described in the Fox Glove Flounce, page 73. These woven bars are also worked in the roses as a filling, and in this case they are added after the rose is worked. Two pairs of bobbins are required to work these bars; as each bar is finished the threads are carried on to the next bar, connecting them once or twice (as necessary) to the lace in between.

Brussels Flounce, Handkerchief, and Lace Edge.

For full size pattern of Brussels Flounce see folding sheet 1.

## BRUSSELS LACE HANDKERCHIEF

This Brussels Handkerchief is 12 inches square and is worked in size 4 thread with a single outline of Bruges cord to correspond.

The cluster of leaves along the border are done in the "raised" work as described on page 100, whilst in the large ornamental scrolls the little fancy twisted braid on the top of the "Half" stitch filling is worked with five pairs of bobbins in "Stem" stitch, described on page 68.

When the lace is completed the centre, which is of gossamer linen cambric, is let in with a fancy open-work stitch, giving it the appearance of drawn thread. First baste the lace to the cambric, using a fine sewing needle and No. 100 sewing cotton. To work the fancy stitch, take up a few threads of the cambric twice in the same place, pulling each stitch rather tight, now take the needle through the edge of the lace and repeat the stitch in the cambric close to the last stitch.

## BRUSSELS LACE EDGE (POINT DE GAZE)

This Lace Edge is 4½ inches wide and worked in size 3 thread, outlined with fine Bruges cord to correspond.

This design is worked entirely in " Cloth " stitch with the exception of the " Half" stitch fillings in the Scrolls. The fine little scallops (indicated on the working Pattern) outlining these scrolls are worked with five pairs of bobbins in " Stem " stitch, which has already been described on page 68. The Point de Gaze Medallions are worked with the needle and let in the lace afterwards, or if preferred, any of the Bobbin Lace stitches given in the book can be substituted for the Point de Gaze with very beautiful effect.

## BRUSSELS LACE FLOUNCE

This Flounce is 8 inches deep and worked in size 4 thread with a single outline of Bruges cord to correspond.

Six pairs of bobbins and one cord are used for the braid outline of the large flowers, which are afterwards filled in with "Half" stitch. The smaller flowers, also the leaves, are worked entirely in "Cloth" stitch.

Five pairs of bobbins and no cord are used for the small scallops bordering the flounce.

The flounce when finished is appliquéd on to fine Brussels Net, and the little dots powdered over the net are then put in with the needle.

The working of these dots, also the method of transferring the lace to the net, is described on page 70.

## FUSCHIA OPERA BAG IN BRUSSELS LACE

The Opera Bag is of dull Rose Silk trimmed aluminium cord. The Fuschia Lace Motif, size 6 inches across by 7 inches deep, is worked in size 4 thread outlined with Bruges cord to correspond. There is no raised work in this design, which is, therefore, not difficult to execute.

The braid outline of the leaves is worked first, with 6 pairs of bobbins and one outline cord. The veins are worked next with 5 pairs of bobbins in " Stem " stitch (described on page 68). When these are completed the entire leaf is then filled in with " Half " stitch, connecting every row to the edge of the leaf and occasionally to the veins; 10 pairs of bobbins are required for the " Half " stitch in the widest portion of the leaf, decreasing to 5 pairs. The leaves with the " Woven Bars " up the middle are worked as described on page 82, except that there is no raised cord in these leaves. After the bars are made, as described on page 82, a single cord bobbin is

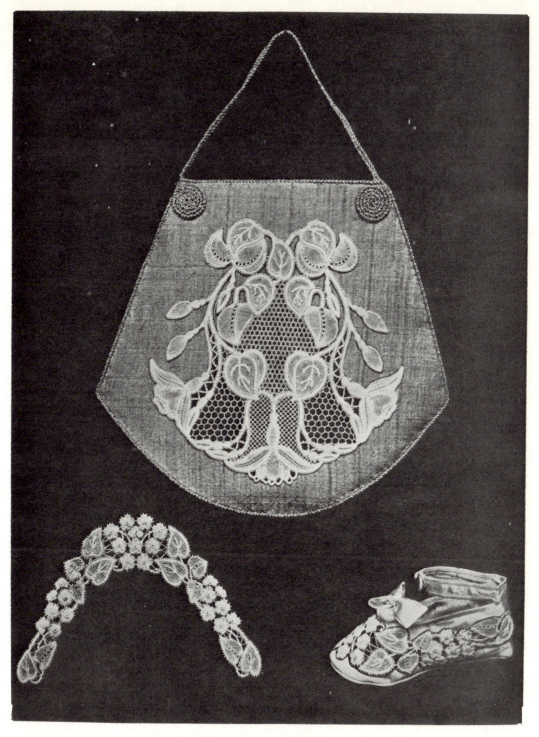

Pair of Baby's Shoes and Opera Bag in Brussels Lace.

For full size pattern of Opera Bag see folding sheet 1.

added, and one side of the leaf worked " Cloth " stitch, the other side " Half " stitch.

A pair of cord bobbins are used in the buds. The upper part of these are worked in " Half " stitch, the cup or lower part in " Cloth " stitch. No cord is used in the stems. The flowers are also worked partly in " Half " stitch and partly in " Cloth " stitch. The centre fuschia has a double vein of " open "-work in the lower petals, these are worked as follows : Commence with seven pairs of bobbins, stick two pins at the top of the leaf, hang three pairs on the right-hand pin one by one and work " Cloth " stitch with each, twist the two outer pairs twice, take the outside pair round the back of the other pin, hang the remaining four pairs on this pin and work " Cloth " stitch through these with the second pair of the first three pairs, have ready a pair of bobbins wound with cord and pin this down a little way from the top of the leaf, pass the left-hand cord bobbin through the working pair and the right-hand cord through the next four pairs of bobbins ; now return to the working pair at the left hand, twist twice, stick pin in front in the same hole as the commencing pin, " Cloth " stitch with this and the outside pair, twist both pairs twice, pass the chord through the inner pair, work " Cloth " stitch right across to opposite cord, pass this through the working pair, twist twice, stick pin in the same hole as the commencing pin at this side; "Cloth" stitch, twist both pairs twice, pass the cord, "Cloth" stitch across to the opposite cord from this; now take out the three commencing pins, pull all the threads and cords gently into position so that no loops are left, carefully move the left-hand pin to the extreme tip point of the leaf, twist the working pair twice, stick pin in the same hole as the previous pin which you have just removed; "Cloth" stitch, twist twice, pin the cord firmly down at the tip of leaf to prevent this slipping, pass the cord through the working pair; "Cloth" stitch across to the opposite cord, pass the cord, twist twice, pin in front; "Cloth" stitch, twist both pairs twice, pass the cord through the inner pair; "Cloth" stitch across to the opposite cord, pass this, twist twice, pin opposite last pin and repeat until you arrive at the vein, adding one pair of bobbins on each of the next three rows to make 10 pairs. As soon as you arrive at the vein indicated on the working Pattern, start to make the double row of open-work as follows: "Cloth" stitch through 3 pairs, twist the working pair three times, "Cloth" stitch through 1 pair, twist the working pair three times, "Cloth" stitch through 3 pairs; repeat this every row to the end of the vein.

The Fillings employed in this Motif (which can, by the way, be used for a variety of purposes, and makes handsome inlet for Frocks, &c.) are the Fine Honeycomb in the centre, the Hexagon Net and Reseau. The working of these Fillings are described in detail in the book.

N

## BABY'S SHOES IN BRUSSELS LACE

The little May Blossom lace shoes are mounted on pale blue silk. They are worked in size 4 thread, outlined with fine Bruges cord to correspond. Six pairs of bobbins and one outline cord are used for the flowers, which are worked in " Cloth " stitch. The leaves and stems are worked as described in the Fuschia Opera Bag. The lace being perfectly shaped to fit the shoe, it is merely necessary to attach this when completed very lightly to the silk Shoes.

| Hexagon Net. | Spot Insertion (curved). | Small Mesh Net. |
| Old Flandres Stitch. | Woven Bar Filling. | Piquè Filling. |
| Fine Honeycomb Stitch. | Spot Insertion (straight). | Large Mesh Net. |

## FANCY STITCHES AND FILLINGS

The directions for working these beautiful and rare Fillings are given in detail in the different Laces in which they are introduced in this book.

All these stitches can be used in a variety of ways and are a distinct addition to the lace, not only in point of interest, but they enhance the beauty and value of the work to a very great degree.

Good taste and judgment, however, must be exercised in arranging the number and position of the different Fillings so as to blend with the character of the Lace and the style of the Design.

The Fancy Net Stitches, of which we give four varieties, " Reseau " (page 53), " Large Mesh " (page 162), " Small Mesh " (page 163), and " Hexagon " (page 125), are used to fill entire backgrounds, as well as smaller spaces; a blend of two or more different net stitches are very effective for the former.

The " Piquè." Filling (page 157) is a strikingly handsome stitch for bold spaces.

The "*Fine* Honeycomb" (page 150), with its delicately fine effects, is suited for smaller spaces, although, like the " Woven Bar" and " Old Flandres" Fillings (pages 143 and 162), it is equally adaptable to large or small spaces.

The " Spot Insertion" has a most enriching effect on all narrow spaces, straight or curved. The directions given on pages 137 to 143 apply to either shape. This " Spot Insertion is perhaps the most complicated of all these Fillings to learn, but after it is once mastered it is quite easy to work.

Of course it is understood that the pupil has mastered the simpler but not less beautiful Fillings given in the first volume of ' The Art of Bobbin Lace,' *viz.*, " Reseau," " Honeycomb," " Festoon," " Spider's Web," " Lead," " Diamond," " Double Reseau," and " Rose," before attempting these more complicated Stitches.

THE SCHOOL OF BOBBIN LACE